How to Pray

RUBEN A. TORREY

COSIMOCLASSICS

NEW YORK

all seasons in the Spirit, and watching thereunto in all perseverance and supplication for all the saints."

Note the *alls*: "with *all* prayer," "at *all* seasons," "in *all* perseverance," "for *all* the saints." Note the piling up of strong words, "prayer," "supplication," "perseverance." Note once more the strong expression, "watching thereunto," more literally, "being sleepless thereunto." Paul realized the natural slothfulness of man, and especially his natural slothfulness in prayer. How seldom we pray things through! How often the church and the individual get right up to the verge of a great blessing in prayer and just then let go, get drowsy, and quit. I wish that these words "being sleepless unto prayer" might burn into our hearts. I wish the whole verse might burn into our hearts.

But why is this constant, persistent, sleepless, overcoming prayer so needful?

1. *Because there is a Devil.*

He is cunning, he is mighty, he never rests, he is ever plotting the downfall of the child of God; and if the child of God relaxes in prayer, the Devil will succeed in ensnaring him.

This is the thought of the context. Verse 12 reads: "For our wrestling is not against flesh and blood, but against the principalities, against the

Chapter 1

THE IMPORTANCE OF PRAYER

IN EPHESIANS 6:18 we read words which put the tremendous importance of prayer with startling and overwhelming force:

"Praying always with all prayer and supplication in the Spirit, and watching thereunto with all perseverance and supplication for all saints."

When we stop to weigh the meaning of these words, then note the connection in which they are found, the intelligent child of God is driven to say,

"I must pray, pray, pray. I must put all my energy and all my heart into prayer. Whatever else I do, I must pray."

The Revised Version is, if possible, stronger than the Authorized:

"With all prayer and supplication praying at

Asking God Ernestly

Deep Sincere or Seriousness

CONTENTS

CHAPTER   PAGE

1. THE IMPORTANCE OF PRAYER 7

2. PRAYING TO GOD 30

3. OBEYING AND PRAYING 37

4. PRAYING IN THE NAME OF CHRIST AND
   ACCORDING TO THE WILL OF GOD 44

5. PRAYING IN THE SPIRIT 54

6. ALWAYS PRAYING AND NOT FAINTING 59

7. ABIDING IN CHRIST 64

8. PRAYING WITH THANKSGIVING 70

9. HINDRANCES TO PRAYER 74

10. WHEN TO PRAY 87

11. THE NEED OF A GENERAL REVIVAL 95

12. THE PLACE OF PRAYER BEFORE AND
    DURING REVIVALS 109

It is not necessary that the whole church get to praying to begin with. Great revivals always begin first in the hearts of a few men and women whom God arouses by His Spirit to believe in Him as a living God, as a God who answers prayer, and upon whose heart He lays a burden from which no rest can be found except in importunate crying unto God.

—from *How to Pray*

How to Pray
Cover © 2007 Cosimo, Inc.

For information, address:

Cosimo, P.O. Box 416
Old Chelsea Station
New York, NY 10113-0416

or visit our website at:
www.cosimobooks.com

How to Pray was originally published in 1900.

Cover design by www.kerndesign.net

ISBN: 978-1-60206-423-2

owers, against the world rulers of this darkness, against the spiritual hosts of wickedness in the heavenly places" (R.V.). Then comes verse 13: Wherefore take up the whole armor of God, that e may be able to withstand in the evil day, and, aving done all, to stand" (R.V.). Next follows description of the different parts of the Chrisan's armor, which we are to put on if we are) stand against the Devil and his mighty wiles. 'hen Paul brings all to a climax in verse 18, tellig us that to all else we must add prayer—conant, persistent, untiring, sleepless prayer in the Ioly Spirit, or all else will go for nothing.

2. *Prayer is God's appointed way for obtaining ings, and the great secret of all lack in our exerience, in our life and in our work is neglect of rayer.*

James brings this out very forcibly in chapter and verse 2 of his epistle: "Ye have not because e ask not." These words contain the secret of ie poverty and powerlessness of the average hristian—neglect of prayer.

Many a Christian is asking, "Why is it I make) little progress in my Christian life?"

"Neglect of prayer," God answers. "You have not because you ask not."

Many a minister is asking, "Why is it I see so little fruit from my labors?"

Again God answers, "Neglect of prayer. You have not because you ask not."

Many a Sunday school teacher is asking, "Why is it that I see so few converted in my Sunday school class?"

Still God answers, "Neglect of prayer. You have not because you ask not."

Both ministers and churches are asking, "Why is it that the church of Christ makes so little headway against unbelief and error and sin and worldliness?"

Once more we hear God answering, "Neglect of prayer. You have not because you ask not."

3. *Those men whom God set forth as a pattern of what He expected Christians to be—the apostles—regarded prayer as the most important business of their lives.*

When the multiplying responsibilities of the Early Church crowded in upon them, they "called the multitude of the disciples unto them, and said, It is not reason that we should leave the Word of God, and serve tables. Wherefore, brethren, look ye out among you seven men of honest report, full of the Holy Ghost and wisdom, whom we may appoint over this business. But *we will ve ourselves continually to prayer* and to the inistry of the Word." It is evident from what aul wrote to the churches and to individuals out praying for them, that much of his time id strength and thought were given to prayer Rom. 1:9, R. V.; Eph. 1:15, 16; Col. 1:9, . V.; I Thess. 3:10; II Tim. 1:3, R. V.) All the mighty men of God outside the Bible ve been men of prayer. They have differed om one another in many things, but in this they ve been alike.

4. *Prayer occupied a very prominent place and 'ayed a very important part in the earthly life : our Lord.*

Turn, for example, to Mark 1:35. "And in ie morning, rising up a great while before day, went out, and departed into a solitary place, d there prayed." The preceding day had been very busy and exciting one, but Jesus shortened ie hours of needed sleep that He might arise rly and give Himself to more sorely needed :ayer.

Turn again to Luke 6:12, where we read, "And came to pass in those days that he went out into mountain to pray, and continued all night in yer to God." Our Saviour found it necessary occasion to take a whole night for prayer.

The words *pray* and *prayer* are used at least twenty-five times in connection with our Lord in the brief record of His life in the four Gospels, and His praying is mentioned in places where the words are not used. Evidently prayer took much of the time and strength of Jesus; a man or woman who does not spend much time in prayer cannot properly be called a follower of Jesus Christ.

5. *Praying is the most important part of the present ministry of our risen Lord.* This reason for constant, persistent, sleepless, overcoming prayer seems if possible even more forcible.

Christ's ministry did not close with His death. His atoning work was finished then, but when He rose and ascended to the right hand of the Father, He entered upon other work for us just as important in its place as His atoning work. It cannot be divorced from His atoning work; it rests upon that as its basis, but it is necessary to our complete salvation.

What that great present work is, by which He carries our salvation on to completeness, we read in Hebrews 7:25: "Wherefore he is able also to save them to the uttermost that come unto God by him, seeing *he ever liveth to make intercession for them.*" This verse tells us that Jesus is able to save us unto the uttermost, not merely *from*

ιe uttermost, but *unto* the uttermost, unto entire
ιmpleteness, absolute perfection, because He not
erely died, but because He also "ever liveth."
The verse also tells us for what purpose He now
ʒes, "*to make intercession* for us," to pray. Pray-
g is the principal thing He is doing in these
ιys. It is by His prayers that He is saving us.

The same thought is found in Paul's remark-
ιle triumphant challenge in Romans 8:34:
Who is he that shall condemn? It is Christ Je-
ιs that died, yea rather, that was raised from
ιe dead, who is at the right hand of God, *who
so maketh intercession for us*" (R. V.)

If we then are to have fellowship with Jesus
hrist in His present work, we must spend much
e in prayer; we must give ourselves to earnest,
ιnstant, persistent, sleepless, overcoming prayer.
know of nothing that has so impressed me with
sense of the importance of praying at all sea-
ns, being much and constantly in prayer, as the
ιought that that is the principal occupation at
esent of my risen Lord. I want to have fellow-
ip with Him, and to that end I have asked the
ιther whatever else He may make me, to make
e at all events an intercessor, to make me a man
ho knows how to pray, and who spends much
me in prayer.

This ministry of intercession is a glorious and a mighty ministry, and we can all have part in it. The man or the woman who is shut away from the public meeting by sickness can have part in it; the busy mother; the woman who has to take in washing for a living can have part—she can mingle prayers for the saints, and for her pastor, and for the unsaved, and for foreign missionaries, with the soap and water as she bends over the wash-tub, and not do the washing any more poorly on that account; the hard-driven man of business can have part in it, praying as he hurries from duty to duty. But of course we must, if we would maintain this spirit of constant prayer, take time—and take plenty of it—when we shall shut ourselves up in the secret place alone with God for nothing but prayer.

6. *Prayer is the means that God has appointed for our receiving mercy, and obtaining grace to help in time of need.*

Hebrews 4:16 is one of the simplest and sweetest verses in the Bible, "Let us therefore come boldly unto the throne of grace, that we may obtain mercy, and find grace to help in time of need." These words make it very plain that God has appointed a way by which we shall seek and obtain mercy and grace. That way is prayer;

old, confident, outspoken approach to the throne
f grace, the most holy place of God's presence,
vhere our sympathizing High Priest, Jesus Christ,
ias entered in our behalf (vv. 14, 15).

Mercy is what we need, grace is what we must
iave, or all our life and effort will end in com-
ilete failure. Prayer is the way to get them.
There is infinite grace at our disposal, and we
nake it ours experimentally by prayer. Oh, if
ve only realized the fullness of God's grace that
s ours for the asking, its height and depth and
ength and breadth, I am sure that we would
pend more time in prayer. The measure of our
ppropriation of grace is determined by the meas-
ire of our prayers.

Who is there that does not feel that he needs
nore grace? Then ask for it. Be constant and
iersistent in your asking. Be importunate and
intiring in your asking. God delights to have
is "shameless" beggars in this direction; for it
hows our faith in Him, and He is mightily
ileased with faith. Because of our "shameless-
iess" He will rise and give us as much as we need
Luke 11:8). What little streams of mercy and
;race most of us know, when we might know
ivers overflowing their banks!

7. *Prayer in the name of Jesus Christ is the*

way Jesus Christ Himself has appointed for His
disciples to obtain fullness of joy.

He states this simply and beautifully in John
16:24: "Hitherto have ye asked nothing in my
name; ask, and ye shall receive, that your joy may
be fulfilled." "Made full" is the way the Revised
Versions reads. Who is there that does not wish
his joy filled full? Well, the way to have it filled
full is by praying in the name of Jesus. We all
know people whose joy is filled full; indeed, it is
just running over, shining from their eyes; bub-
bling out of their very lips, and running off their
fingertips when they shake hands with you. Coming in contact with them is like coming in contact with an electrical machine charged with glad-
ness. Now people of that sort are always people
that spend much time in prayer.

Why is it that prayer in the name of Christ
brings such fullness of joy? In part, because we
get what we ask. But that is not the only reason,
nor the greatest. It makes God real. When we
ask something definite of God, and He gives it,
how real God becomes! He is right there! It is
blessed to have a God who is real, and not merely
an idea. I remember how once I was taken suddenly and seriously sick all alone in my study. I
dropped upon my knees and cried to God for help.

Instantly all pain left me—I was perfectly well. It seemed as if God stood right there, and had put out His hand and touched me. The joy of the healing was not so great as the joy of meeting God.

There is no greater joy on earth or in Heaven than communion with God, and prayer in the name of Jesus brings us into communion with Him. The Psalmist was surely not speaking only of future blessedness, but also of present blessedness when he said, "In thy presence is fullness of joy" (Ps. 16:11). Oh, the unutterable joy of those moments when in our prayers we really press into the presence of God!

Does someone say, "I have never known any such joy as that in prayer"?

Do you take enough leisure for prayer to actually get into God's presence? Do you really give yourself up to prayer in the time which you do take?

8. *Prayer, in every care and anxiety and need of life, with thanksgiving, is the means that God has appointed for our obtaining freedom from all anxiety, and the peace of God which passeth all understanding.*

"Be careful for nothing," says Paul, "but in everything by prayer and supplication with thanks-

giving let your requests be made known unto
God, and the peace of God which passeth all
understanding, shall keep your hearts and minds
through Christ Jesus" (Phil. 4:6, 7). To many
this seems, at the first glance, the picture of a
life that is beautiful, but beyond the reach of
ordinary mortals; not so at all. The verse tells
us how the life is attainable by every child of
God: "Be careful for nothing," or as the Revised
Version reads, "In nothing be anxious." The re-
mainder of the verse tells us how, and it is very
simple: "But in everything by prayer and supplication with thanksgiving let your requests be
made known unto God." What could be plainer
or more simple than that? Just keep in constant
touch with God, and when any trouble or vex-
ation, great or small, comes up, speak to Him about
it, never forgetting to return thanks for what
He has already done. What will the result be?
"The peace of God which passeth all understanding shall guard your hearts and your thoughts in
Christ Jesus" (R. V.).

That is glorious, and as simple as it is glorious!
Thank God, many are trying it. Don't you know
anyone who is always serene? Perhaps he is a
very stormy man by his natural make-up, but
troubles and conflicts and reverses and bereave-

ments may sweep around him, and the peace of God which passes all understanding guards his heart and his thoughts in Christ Jesus.

We all know such persons. How do they manage it?

Just by prayer, that is all. Those persons who know the deep peace of God, the unfathomable peace that passes all understanding, are always men and women of much prayer.

Some of us let the hurry of our lives crowd prayer out, and what a waste of time and energy and nerve force there is by the constant worry! One night of prayer will save us from many nights of insomnia. Time spent in prayer is not wasted, but time invested at big interest.

9. *Prayer is the method that God Himself has appointed for our obtaining the Holy Spirit.*

Upon this point the Bible is very plain. Jesus says, "If ye then, being evil, know how to give good gifts unto your children, how much more shall your heavenly Father give the Holy Spirit to them that ask him?" (Luke 11:13). Men are telling us in these days, very good men too, "You must not pray for the Holy Spirit." But what are they going to do with the plain statement of Jesus Christ, "How much more will your heav-

20

enly Father give the Holy Spirit *to them that ask him?*"

Some years ago when an address on the baptism with the Holy Spirit was announced, a brother came to me before the address and said with much feeling,

"Be sure and tell them not to pray for the Holy Spirit."

"I will surely not tell them that, for Jesus says, 'How much more shall your heavenly Father give the Holy Spirit to them that ask him.'"

"Oh, yes," he replied, "but that was before Pentecost."

"How about Acts 4:31? Was that before Pentecost, or after?"

"After of course."

"Read it."

"'And when *they had prayed*, the place was shaken where they were assembled together; and they were all *filled with the Holy Ghost*, and they spake the word of God with boldness.'"

"How about Acts 8:15? Was that before Pentecost or after?"

"After."

"Please read."

"'Who, when they were come down, *prayed* for them, that they might receive the Holy Ghost.'"

He made no answer. What could he answer? It is plain as day in the Word of God that before Pentecost and after, the first baptism and the subsequent fillings with the Holy Spirit were received in answer to definite prayer. Experience also teaches this.

Doubtless many have received the Holy Spirit the moment of their surrender to God before there was time to pray; but how many there are who know that their first definite baptism with the Holy Spirit came while they were on their knees or faces before God, alone or in company with others, and who again and again since that have been filled with the Holy Spirit in the place of prayer!

I know this as definitely as I know that my thirst has been quenched while I was drinking water. Early one morning in the Chicago Avenue Church prayer room, where several hundred people had been assembled a number of hours in prayer, the Holy Spirit fell so manifestly, and the whole place was so filled with His presence, that no one could speak or pray, but sobs of joy filled the place. Men went out of that room to different parts of the country, taking trains that very morning, and reports soon came back of the outpouring of God's Holy Spirit in answer to prayer. Others went out into the city with the blessing of God upon them. This is only one instance among many that might be cited from personal experience.

If we would only spend more time in prayer, there would be more fullness of the Spirit's power in our work. Many and many a man who once worked unmistakably in the power of the Holy Spirit is now filling the air with empty shoutings, and beating it with his meaningless gesticulations, because he has let prayer be crowded out. We must spend much time on our knees before God, if we are to continue in the power of the Holy Spirit.

10. *Prayer is the means that Christ has appointed whereby our hearts shall not become overcharged with surfeiting and drunkenness and cares of this life, and so the day of Christ's return come upon us suddenly as a snare.*

One of the most interesting and solemn passages upon prayer in the Bible is along this line (Luke 21:34-36). "Take heed to yourselves, lest at any time your hearts be overcharged with surfeiting and drunkenness and cares of this life, and so that day come upon you unawares. For as a snare shall it come on all them that dwell on the face of the whole earth. Watch ye therefore, and *pray al-*

ways, that ye may be accounted worthy to escape all these things that shall come to pass, and to stand before the Son of man." According to this passage there is only one way in which we can be prepared for the coming of the Lord when He appears, that is, through much prayer.

The coming again of Jesus Christ is a subject that is awakening much interest and much discussion in our day; but it is one thing to be interested in the Lord's return, and to talk about it, and quite another thing to be prepared for it. We live in an atmosphere that has a constant tendency to unfit us for Christ's coming. The world tends to draw us down by its gratifications and by its cares. There is only one way by which we can rise triumphant above these things—by constant watching unto prayer, that is, by sleeplessness unto prayer. *Watch* in this passage is the same strong word used in Ephesians 6:18, and *always* the same strong phrase *in every season.* The man who spends little time in prayer, who is not steadfast and constant in prayer, will not be ready for the Lord when He comes. But we may be ready. How? Pray! Pray! Pray!

11. *Because of what prayer accomplishes.* Much has really been said upon that already, but there is much also that should be added.

a) Prayer promotes our spiritual growth as almost nothing else, indeed as nothing else but Bible study; and true prayer and true Bible study go hand in hand.

It is through prayer that my sin is brought to light, my most hidden sin. As I kneel before God and pray, "Search me, O God, and know my heart: try me, and know my thoughts: and see if there be any wicked way in me" (Ps. 139:23, 24), God shoots the penetrating rays of His light into the innermost recesses of my heart, and the sins I never suspected are brought to view. In answer to prayer, God washes me from mine iniquity and cleanses me from my sin (Ps. 51:2). In answer to prayer my eyes are opened to behold wondrous things out of God's Word (Ps. 119:18). In answer to prayer I get wisdom to know God's way (James 1:5) and strength to walk in it. As I meet God in prayer and gaze into His face, I am changed into His own image from glory to glory (II Cor. 3:18). Each day of true prayer life finds me liker to my glorious Lord.

John Welch, son-in-law to John Knox, was one of the most faithful men of prayer this world ever saw. He counted that day ill-spent in which seven or eight hours were not used alone with God in prayer and the study of His Word. An

ld man speaking of him after his death said,
'He was a type of Christ."

How came he to be so like his Master?

His prayer life explains the mystery.

b) Prayer brings power into our work.

If we wish power for any work to which God
:alls us, be it preaching, teaching, personal work,
ır the rearing of our children, we can get it by
:arnest prayer.

A woman with a little boy who was perfectly
ncorrigible, once came to me in desperation and
aid:

"What shall I do with him?"

I asked, "Have you ever tried prayer?"

She said that she had prayed for him, she
hought. I asked if she had made his conversion
ınd his character a matter of definite, expectant
ırayer. She replied that she had not been defnite
n the matter. She began that day, and at once
here was a marked change in the child, and he
;rew up into Christian manhood.

How many a Sunday school teacher has taught
'or months and years, and seen no real fruit from
ıis labors, and then has learned the secret of inter-
:ession, and by earnest pleading with God, has
een his scholars brought one by one to Christ!
Iow many a poor preacher has become a mighty

man of God by casting away his confidence in his own ability and gifts, and giving himself up to God to wait upon Him for the power that comes from on high! John Livingstone spent a night, with some others likeminded, in prayer to God and religious conversation, and when he preached next day in the Kirk of Shotts five hundred people were converted, or dated some definite uplift in their life to that occasion. Prayer and power are inseparable.

c) Prayer avails for the conversion of others.

There are few converted in this world unless in connection with someone's prayers. I formerly thought that no human being had anything to do with my own conversion, for I was not converted in church or Sunday school, or in personal conversation with anyone. I was awakened in the middle of the night and converted. As far as I can remember I had not the slightest thought of being converted, or of anything of that character, when I went to bed and fell asleep; but I was awakened in the middle of the night and converted probably inside of five minutes. A few minutes before I was about as near eternal perdition as one gets. I had one foot over the brink and was trying to get the other one over. I say I thought no human being had anything to do

ith it, but I had forgotten my mother's prayers,
id I afterwards learned that one of my college
assmates had chosen me as one to pray for until
was saved.

Prayer often avails where everything else fails.
ow utterly all of Monica's efforts and entreaties
iiled with her son! But her prayers' prevailed
th God, and the dissolute youth became St.
ugustine, the mighty man of God. By prayer
ie bitterest enemies of the gospel have become
s most valiant defenders, the greatest scoundrels
ie truest sons of God, and the vilest women the
urest saints. Oh, the power of prayer to reach
own, down, down where hope itself seems vain,
id lift men and women up, up, up into fellow-
iip with and likeness to God! It is simply won-
erful! How little we appreciate this marvelous
reapon!

d) Prayer brings blessings to the Church.

The history of the Church has always been a
istory of grave difficulties to overcome. The
)evil hates the Church and seeks in every way to
lock its progress; now by false doctrine, again by
division, again by inward corruption of life. But
y prayer, a clear way can be made through every-
hing. Prayer will root out heresy, allay misunder-
:anding, sweep away jealousies and animosities,

obliterate immoralities, and bring in the full tide of God's reviving grace. History abundantly proves this. In the hour of darkest portent, when the case of the Church, local or universal, has seemed beyond 'hope, believing men and believing women have met together and cried to God and the answer has come.

It was so in the days of Knox, it was so in the days of Wesley and Whitefield, it was so in the day of Edwards and Brainerd, it was so in the days of Finney, it was so in the days of the great revival of 1857 in this country and of 1859 in Ireland. And it will be so again in your day and mine! Satan has marshalled his forces. Christian science with its false Christ—a woman—lifts high its head. Others making great pretentions of apostolic methods, but covering the rankest dishonesty and hypocrisy with these pretentions speak with loud assurance. Christians equally loyal to the great fundamental truths of the Gospel are glowering at one another with a Devil-sent suspicion. The world, the flesh and the Devil are holding high carnival. It is now a dark day, but —now "it is time for thee, Lord, to work; for they have made void thy law" (Ps. 119:126). And He is getting ready to work, and now He is list-

ing for the voice of prayer. Will He hear it?
ill He hear it from you? Will He hear it from
e Church as a body? I believe He will.

Chapter 2

PRAYING TO GOD

WE HAVE SEEN something of the tremendous importance and the resistless power of prayer, and now we come directly to the question—how to pray with power.

1. In the twelfth chapter of the Acts of the Apostles we have the record of a prayer that prevailed with God, and brought to pass great results. In the fifth verse of this chapter, the manner and method of this prayer is described in few words:

"Prayer was made without ceasing of the church *unto God* for him."

The first thing to notice in this verse is the brief expression "unto God." The prayer that has power is the prayer that is offered unto God.

But some will say, "Is not all prayer unto God?"

No. Very much of so-called prayer, both pub-
c and private, is not unto God. In order that
prayer should be really unto God, there must be
definite and conscious approach to God when we
ray; we must have a definite and vivid realiza-
on that God is bending over us and listening as
e pray. In very much of our prayer there is
ally but little thought of God. Our mind is
ken up with the thought of what we need, and
 not occupied with the thought of the mighty
nd loving Father of whom we are seeking it.
)ftentimes it is the case that we are occupied
either with the need nor with the One to whom
e are praying, but our mind is wandering here
nd there throughout the world. There is no power
 that sort of prayer. But when we really come
to God's presence, really meet Him face to face
 the place of prayer, really seek the things that
e desire *from Him*, then there is power.

If, then, we would pray aright, the first things
hat we should do is to see that we really get an
udience with God, that we really get into His
ery presence. Before a word of petition is of-
red, we should have the definite and vivid con-
iousness that we are talking to God, and should
elieve that He is listening to our petition and is
oing to grant the thing that we ask of Him. This

is only possible by the Holy Spirit's power, so we should look to the Holy Spirit to really lead us into the presence of God, and should not be hasty in words until He has actually brought us there.

One night a very active Christian man dropped into a little prayer meeting that I was leading. Before we knelt to pray, I said something like the above, telling all the friends to be sure before they prayed, and while they were praying, that they really were in God's presence, that they had the thought of Him definitely in mind, and to be more taken up with Him than with their petition. A few days after I met this same gentleman, and he said that this simple thought was entirely new to him, that it had made prayer an entirely new experience to him.

If then we would pray aright, these two little words must sink deep into our heart, *unto God*.

2. The second secret of effective praying is found in the same verse, in the words, *without ceasing*.

In the Revised Version, "without ceasing" is rendered "earnestly." Neither rendering gives the full force of the Grek. The word means literally, "stretched-out-ed-ly." It is a pictorial word, and wonderfully expressive. It represents the soul on a stretch of earnest and intense desire. "Intensely"

ould perhaps come as near translating it as any
nglish word. It is the word used of our Lord in
uke 22:44 where it is said, "He prayed more
irnestly, and his sweat was as it were great drops
f blood falling down to the ground."

We read in Hebrews 5:7 that "in the days of
is flesh" Christ "offered up prayers and suppli-
itions with strong crying and tears." In Romans
5:30 Paul beseeches the saints in Rome to *strive*
)gether with him in their prayers. The word
·anslated *strive* means primarily to contend as in
:hletic games or in a fight. In other words, the
rayer that prevails with God is the prayer into
hich we put our whole soul, stretching out to-
·ard God in intense and agonizing desire. Much of
ir modern prayer has no power in it because
ιere is no heart in it. We rush into God's pres-
ιce, run through a string of petitions, jump up
ιd go out. If someone should ask us an hour
fterward for what we prayed, oftentimes we
ould not tell. If we put so little heart into our
rayers, we cannot expect God to put much heart
to answering them.

We hear much in our day of the rest of faith,
ut there is no such thing as the fight of faith in
rayer as well as in effort. Those who would have
s think that they have attained to some sublime

height of faith and trust because they never know any agony of conflict or of prayer, have surely gotten beyond their Lord, and beyond the mightiest victors for God, both in effort and prayer, that the ages of Christian history have known. When we learn to come to God with an intensity of desire that wrings the soul, then shall we know a power in prayer that most of us do not know now.

But how shall we attain to this earnestness in prayer?

Not by trying to work ourselves up into it. The true method is explained in Romans 8:26: "And in like manner the Spirit also helpeth our infirmity: for we know not how to pray as we ought; but the Spirit himself maketh intercession for us with groanings which cannot be uttered" (R. V.) The earnestness that we work up in the energy of the flesh is a repulsive thing. The earnestness wrought in us by the Holy Spirit is pleasing to God. Here again, if we would pray aright, we must look to the Spirit of God to teach us to pray.

It is in this connection that fasting comes. In Daniel 9:3 we read that Daniel set his face "unto the Lord God, to seek by prayer and supplications, with fasting, and sackcloth, and ashes." There are those who think that fasting belongs to the old dispensation; but when we look at Acts 14:23 and Acts 13:2, 3, we find that it was practiced by the earnest men of the apostolic day.

If we would pray with power, we should pray with fasting. This of course does not mean that we should fast every time we pray; but there are times of emergency or special crisis in work or in our individual lives, when men of downright earnestness will withdraw themselves even from the gratification of natural appetites that would be perfectly proper under other circumstances, that they may give themselves up wholly to prayer. There is a peculiar power in such prayer. Every great crisis in life and work should be met in that way. There is nothing pleasing to God in our giving up in a purely Pharisaic and legal way things which are pleasant, but there is power in that downright earnestness and determination to obtain in prayer the things of which we sorely feel our need, that leads us to put away everything, even things in themselves most right and necessary, that we may set our faces to find God, and obtain blessings from Him.

3. A third secret of right praying is also found in this same verse, Acts 12:5. It appears in the three words, *of the church*.

There is power in *united prayer*. Of course

there is power in the prayer of an individual but there is vastly increased power in united prayer. God delights in the unity of His people, and seeks to emphasize it in every way, and so He pronounces a special blessing upon united prayer. We read in Matthew 18:19, "If two of you shall agree on earth as touching anything that they shall ask, it shall be done for them of my Father which is in heaven." This unity, however, must be real. The passage just quoted does not say that if two shall agree in asking, but if two shall agree *as touching* anything they shall ask. Two persons might agree to ask for the same thing, and yet there be no real agreement as touching the thing they asked. One might ask it because he really desired it, the other might ask it simply to please his friend. But where there is real agreement, where the Spirit of God brings two believers into perfect harmony as concerning that which they may ask of God, where the Spirit lays the same burden on two hearts, in all such prayer there is absolutely irresistible power.

Chapter 3

OBEYING AND PRAYING

1.   One of the most significant verses in the Bible on prayer is I John 3:22. John says, "And whatsoever we ask, we receive of him, because we keep his commandments and do those things that are pleasing in his sight."

What an astounding statement! John says, in so many words, that everything he asked for he got. How many of us can say this: "Whatsoever I ask I receive"? But John explains why this was so, "Because we keep his commandments, and do those things that are pleasing in his sight." In other words, the one who expects God to do as he asks Him, must on his part *do whatever God bids him.* If we give a listening ear to all God's commands to us, He will give a listening ear to all our petitions to Him. If, on the other hand, we turn a deaf ear to His precepts, He will be likely

to turn a deaf ear to our prayers. Here we find
the secret of much unanswered prayer. We are
not listening to God's Word, and therefore He is
not listening to our petitions.

I was once speaking to a woman who had been
a professed Christian, but had given it all up. I
asked her why she was not a Christian still. She
replied, because she did not believe the Bible. I
asked her why she did not believe the Bible.

"Because I have tried its promises and found
them untrue."

"Which promises?"

"The promises about prayer."

"Which promises about prayer?"

"Does it not say in the Bible, 'Whatsoever ye
ask believing ye shall receive?' "

"It says something nearly like that."

"Well, I asked fully expecting to get and did
not receive, so the promise failed."

"Was the promise made to you?"

"Why, certainly, it is made to all Christians, is
it not?"

"No, God carefully defines who the *ye's* are
whose believing prayers He agrees to answer."

I then turned her to I John 3:22, and read the
description of those whose prayers had power with
God.

"Now," I said, "were you keeping His com-
andments and doing those things which are
leasing in His sight?"

She frankly confessed that she was not, and soon
ıme to see that the real difficulty was not with
od's promises, but with herself.   That is the
ifficulty with many an unanswered prayer to-
ıy: the one who offers it is not obedient.

If we would have power in prayer, we must be
ırnest students of His Word to find out what His
ill regarding us is, and then having found it,
o it.   One unconfessed act of disobedience on
ur part will shut the ear of God against many
etitions.

2.   But this verse goes beyond the mere keeping
f God's commandments.   John tells us that we
ıust *do those things that are pleasing in His sight.*

There are many things which it would be pleas-
ıg to God for us to do which He has not spe-
ifically commanded us.   A true child is not con-
ınt with merely doing those things which his
ıther specifically commands him to do.   He stu-
ies to know his father's will, and if he thinks that
here is any thing that he can do that would please
is father, he does it gladly, though his father has
ever given him any specific order to do it.   So
: is with the true child of God.   He does not

ask merely whether certain things are commanded or certain things forbidden. He studies to know is Father's will in all things.

There are many Christians today who are doing things that are not pleasing to God, and leaving undone things which would be pleasing to God. When you speak to them about these things they will confront you at once with the question, "Is there any command in the Bible not to do this thing?" And if you cannot show them the verse in which the matter in question is plainly forbidden, they think they are under no obligation whatever to give it up; but a true child of God does not demand a specific command. If we make it our study to find out and do the things which are pleasing to God, He will make it His study to do the things which are pleasing to us. Here again we find the explanation of much unanswered prayer: We are not making it the study of our lives to know what would please our Father and so our prayers are not answered.

Take as an illustration of questions that are constantly coming up, the matter of theater-going, dancing and the use of tobacco. Many who are indulging in these things will ask you triumphantly if you speak against them, "Does the Bible say, 'Thou shalt not go to the theater'?" "Does the

Bible say, 'Thou shalt not dance'?" "Does the
Bible say, 'Thou shalt not smoke'?" That is not
the question. The question is, Is our heavenly
Father well pleased when He sees one of His children in the theater, at the dance, or smoking?
That is a question for each to decide for himself,
prayerfully, seeking light from the Holy Spirit.
"Where is the harm in these things?" many ask.
It is aside from our purpose to go into the general
question but beyond a doubt there is great harm
in many a case; they rob our prayers of power.

3. Psalm 145:18 throws a great deal of light
on the question of how to pray: "The Lord is
nigh unto all them that call upon him, to all that
call upon him in truth."

That little expression *in truth* is worthy of
study. If you will take your concordance and go
through the Bible, you will find that this expression means "in reality," "in sincerity." The prayer
that God answers is the prayer that is real,
the prayer that asks for something that is sin-
cerely desired.

Much prayer is insincere. People ask for things
which they do not wish. Many a woman is praying for the conversion of her husband who does
not really wish her husband to be converted. She
thinks that she does, but if she knew what would

be involved in the conversion of her husband, how it would necessitate an entire revolution in his manner of doing business, and how consequently it would reduce their income and make necessary an entire change in their method of living, the real prayer of her heart would be, if she were to be sincere with God:

"O God, do not convert my husband."

She does not wish his conversion at so great cost.

Many a church is praying for a revival that does not really desire a revival. They think they do, for to their minds a revival means an increase of membership, an increase of income, an increase of reputation among the churches; but if they knew what a real revival meant, what a searching of hearts on the part of professed Christians would be involved, what a radical transformation of individual, domestic and social life would be brought about, and many other things that would come to pass if the Spirit of God was poured out in reality and power; if all this were known the real cry of the church would be:

"O God, keep us from having a revival."

Many a minister is praying for the baptism with the Holy Spirit who does not really desire it. He thinks he does, for the baptism with the Spirit means to him new joy, new power in preaching the

ord, a wider reputation among men, a larger
:ominence in the church of Christ. But if he
ıderstood what a baptism with the Holy Spirit
:ally involved, how for example it would neces-
rily bring him into antagonism with the world,
ıd with unspiritual Christians, how it would
ıuse his name to be "cast out as evil," how it
˙ght necessitate his leaving a good comfortable
ving and going down to work in the slums, or
˙en in some foreign land; if he understood all
ıis, his prayer quite likely would be—if he were
ı express the real wish of his heart—"O God,
.ve me from being baptized with the Holy
host."

But when we do come to the place where we
:ally desire the conversion of friends at any cost,
:ally desire the outpouring of the Holy Spirit
hatever it may involve, really desire the baptism
ith the Holy Ghost come what may, where we
esire anything "in truth" and then call upon
:od for it "in truth," God is going to hear.

Chapter 4

PRAYING IN THE NAME OF CHRIST AND ACCORDING TO THE WILL OF GOD

1. It was a wonderful word about prayer that Jesus spoke to His disciples on the night before His crucifixion: "Whatsoever ye shall ask *in my name*, that will I do, that the Father may be glorified in the Son. If ye shall ask anything in my name, I will do it."

Prayer in the name of Christ has power with God. God is well pleased .with His Son Jesus Christ. He hears Him always, and He also hears always the prayer that is really in His name. There is a fragrance in the name of Christ that makes acceptable to God every prayer that bears it.

But what is it to pray in the name of Christ?

Many explanations have been attempted that to

rdinary minds do not explain. But there is noth-
ig mystical or mysterious about this expression.
f one will go through the Bible and examine all
ie passages in which the expression "in my name"
r "in his name" or synonymous expressions are
sed, he will find that it means just about what it
oes in modern usage. If I go to a bank and hand
i a check with my name signed to it, I ask of that
ank *in my own name*. If I have money deposited
i that bank, the check will be cashed; if not, it
rill not be. If, however, I go to a bank with
imebody's else name signed to the check, I am
sking *in his name*, and it does not matter whether
have money in that bank or any other, if the
erson whose name is signed to the check has
ioney there, the check will be cashed.

If, for example, I should go to the First Na-
ional Bank of Chicago, and present a check which
had signed for $50.00, the paying teller would
iy to me:

"Why, Mr. Torrey, we cannot cash that. You
ave no money in this bank."

But if I should go to the First National Bank
rith a check for $50.00 made payable to me, and
gned by one of the large depositors in that bank,
hey would not ask whether I had money in that

bank or in any bank, but would honor the check at once.

It is like going to the bank of Heaven when I go to God in prayer. I have nothing deposited there; I have absolutely no credit there, and if I go in my own name I will get absolutely nothing; but Jesus Christ has unlimited credit in Heaven, and He has granted to me the privilege of going to the bank with His name on my checks; and when I thus go, my prayers will be honored to any extent.

To pray then in the name of Christ is to pray on the ground, not of my credit, but His; to renounce the thought that I have any claims on God whatever, and approach Him on the ground of Christ's claims. Praying in the name of Christ is not merely adding the phrase, "I ask these things in Jesus' name," to my prayer. I may put that phrase in my prayer and really be resting in my own merit all the time. On the other hand, I may omit that phrase but really be resting in the merit of Christ all the time. But when I really do approach God, not on the ground of my merit, but on the ground of Christ's merit, not on the ground of my goodness, but on the ground of the atoning blood (Heb. 10:19), God will hear me. Very much of our modern prayer is vain because men approach God imagining that they have some claim upon God whereby He is under obligation to answer their prayers.

Years ago when Mr. Moody was young in Christian work, he visited a town in Illinois. A judge in the town was an infidel. This judge's wife besought Mr. Moody to call upon her husband, but Mr. Moody replied:

"I cannot talk with your husband. I am only an uneducated young Christian, and your husband is a book infidel."

But the wife should not take *no* for an answer, so Mr. Moody made the call. The clerks in the outer office tittered as the young salesman from Chicago went in to talk with the scholarly judge.

The conversation was short. Mr. Moody said:

"Judge, I can't talk with you. You are a book infidel and I have no learning, but I simply want to say if you are ever converted, I want you to let me know."

The judge replied: "Yes, young man, if I am ever converted I will let you know. Yes, I will let you know."

The conversation ended. The clerks tittered still louder when the zealous young Christian left the office, but the judge was converted within a year. Mr. Moody visiting the town again asked the judge to explain how it came about. The judge said:

"One night, when my wife was at prayer meeting I began to grow very uneasy and miserable. I did not know what was the matter with me, but finally retired before my wife came home. I could not sleep all that night. I got up early, told my wife that I would eat no breakfast, and went down to the office. I told the clerks they could take a holiday, and shut myself up in the inner office. I kept growing more and more miserable, and finally I got down and asked God to forgive my sins, but I would not say 'for Jesus' sake,' for I was a Unitarian and I did not believe in the atonement. I kept praying 'God forgive my sins'; but no answer came. At last in desperation I cried, 'O God, for Christ's sake forgive my sins,' and found peace at once."

The judge had no access to God until he came in the name of Christ, but when he thus came, he was heard and answered at once.

2. Great light is thrown upon the subject "How to Pray" by I John 5:14, 15: "And this is the boldness which we have toward him, that if we ask anything *according to his will*, he heareth us: and if we know that he heareth us what-

)ever we ask, we know that we have the petitions
which we have asked of him" (R. V.)

This passage teaches us plainly that if we are to
pray aright, we must pray according to God's will,
then will we beyond a peradventure get the thing
we ask of Him.

But can we know the will of God? Can we
know that any specific prayer is according to His
will?

We most surely can.

How?

a) First by the Word. God has revealed His
will in His Word. When anything is definitely
promised in the Word of God, we know that it is
His will to give that thing. If then when I pray,
I can find some definite promise of God's Word and
lay that promise before God, I know that He hears
me, and if I know that He hears me, I know that
I have the petition that I have asked of Him. For
example, when I pray for wisdom I know that it
is the will of God to give me wisdom, for He says
so in James 1:5: "If any of you lack wisdom,
let him ask of God, that giveth to all men liberally, and upbraideth not; and it shall be given
him." So when I ask for wisdom I know that the
prayer is heard, and that wisdom will be given me.
In like manner when I pray for the Holy Spirit

I know from Luke 11:13 that it is God's will, that my prayer is heard, and that I have the petition that I have asked of Him: "If ye then, being evil, know how to give good gifts unto your children, how much more shall your heavenly Father give the Holy Spirit to them that ask him?"

Some years ago a minister came to me at the close of an address on prayer at a Y. M. C. A. Bible school, and said,

"You have produced upon those young men the impression that they can ask for definite things and get the very things that they ask."

I replied that I did not know whether that was the impression that I had produced or not, but that was certainly the impression that I desired to produce.

"But," he replied, "that is not right. We cannot be sure, for we don't know God's will."

I turned him at once to James 1:5, read it and said to him, "Is it not God's will to give us wisdom, and if you ask for wisdom do you not know that you are going to get it?"

"Ah!" he said, "we don't know what wisdom is."

I said, "No, if we did, we would not need to ask; but whatever wisdom may be, don't you know that you will get it?"

Certainly is it our privilege to know. When we have a specific promise in the Word of God, if we doubt that it is God's will, or if we doubt that God will do the thing that we ask, we make God a liar.

Here is one of the greatest secrets of prevailing prayer: To study the Word to find what God's will is as revealed there in the promises, and then simply take these promises and spread them out before God in prayer with the absolutely unwavering expectation that He will do what He has promisd in His Word.

b) But there is still another way in which we may know the will of God, that is, by the teaching of His Holy Spirit. There are many things that we need from God which are not covered by any specific promise, but we are not left in ignorance of the will of God even then. In Romans 8:26, 27 we are told, "And in like manner the Spirit also helpeth our infirmity: for we know not how to pray as we ought; but the Spirit himself maketh intercession for us with groanings which cannot be uttered; and he that searcheth the hearts knoweth what is the mind of the Spirit, because he maketh intercession for the saints *according to the will of God*" (R. V.) Here we are distinctly told that the Spirit of God prays in us,

draws out our prayer, in the line of God's will.
When we are thus led out by the Holy Spirit in
any direction, to pray for any given object, we
may do it in all confidence that it is God's will,
and that we are to get the very thing we ask of
Him, even though there is no specific promise to
cover the case.   Often God by His Spirit lays upon us a heavy burden of prayer for some given
individual. We cannot rest, we pray for him with
groanings which cannot be uttered.   Perhaps the
man is entirely beyond our reach, but God hears
the prayer and in many a case it is not long before
we hear of his definite conversion.

The passage I John 5:14, 15, is one of the most
abused passages in the Bible: "This is *the confidence* that we have in him, that, if we ask anything according to his will, he heareth us; and if
we know that he hear us, whatsoever we ask, we
know that we have the petitions that we desired
of him."   The Holy Spirit beyond a doubt put it
into the Bible to encourage our faith.   It begins
with "This is *the confidence* that we have in him,"
and closes with "*We know* that we have the petitions that we desired of him"; but one of the most
frequent usages of this passage, which was so manifestly given to beget confidence, is to introduce
an element of uncertainty into our prayers. Often-

times when one waxes confident in prayer, some cautious brother will come and say:

"Now, don't be too confident. If it is God's will He will do it. You should put in, 'If it be Thy will.'"

Doubtless there are many times when we do not know the will of God, and in all prayer submission to the excellent will of God should underlie it; but when we know God's will, there need be no *if*'s; and this passage was not put into the Bible in order that we might introduce *if*'s into all our prayers, but in order that we might throw our *if*'s to the wind, and have *"confidence"* and *"know* that we have the petitions which we have asked of him."

Chapter 5

PRAYING IN THE SPIRIT

1. Over and over again in what has already been said, we have seen our dependence upon the Holy Spirit in prayer. This comes out very defnitely in Ephesians 6:18, "Praying always with all prayer and supplication *in the Spirit*"; and in Jude 20, "Praying *in the Holy Ghost*." Indeed the whole secret of prayer is found in these three words, *in the Spirit*. It is the prayer that God the Holy Spirit inspires that God the Father answers.

The disciples did not know how to pray as they ought, so they came to Jesus and said, "Lord, teach us to pray." We know not how to pray as we ought, but we have another Teacher and Guide right at hand to help us (John 14:16, 17). "The Spirit helpeth our infirmity" (Rom. 8:26, R. V.). He teaches us how to pray. True prayer is prayer n the Spirit; that is, the prayer the Spirit inspires nd directs. When we come into God's presence ve should recognize "our infirmity," our ignor- nce of what we should pray for or how we should ıray for it, and in the consciousness of our utter nability to pray aright we should look up to the Ioly Spirit, casting ourselves utterly upon Him o direct our prayers, to lead out our desires and o guide our utterance of them.

Nothing can be more foolish in prayer than to ush heedlessly into God's presence and ask the irst thing that comes into our mind, or that some houghtless friend has asked us to pray for. When ve first come into God's presence we should be ilent before Him. We should look up to Him to end His Holy Spirit to teach us how to pray. We nust wait for the Holy Spirit, and surrender our- elves to the Spirit, then we shall pray aright.

Oftentimes when we come to God in prayer, we lo not feel like praying. What shall one do in uch a case? Cease praying until he does feel like t? Not at all. When we feel least like praying s the time when we most need to pray. We hould wait quietly before God and tell Him how :old and prayerless our hearts are, and look up to Iim and trust Him and expect Him to send the Ioly Spirit to warm our hearts and draw them out in prayer. It will not be long before the glow of the Spirit's presence will fill our hearts, and we will begin to pray with freedom, directness, earnestness and power. Many of the most blessed seasons of prayer I have ever known have begun with a feeling of utter deadness and prayerlessness; but in my helplessness and coldness I have cast myself upon God, and looked to Him to send His Holy Spirit to teach me to pray, and He has done it.

When we pray in the Spirit, we will pray for the right things and in the right way. There will be joy and power in our prayer.

2. If we are to pray with power we must pray *with faith*. In Mark 11:24 Jesus says, "Therefore I say unto you, What things soever ye desire, when ye pray, believe that ye receive them, and ye shall have them." No matter how positive any promise of God's Word may be, we will not enjoy it in actual experience unless we confidently expect its fulfillment in answer to our prayer. "If any of you lack wisdom," says James, "let him ask of God that giveth to all men liberally, and upbraideth not; and it shall be given him." Now that promise is as positive as a promise can be, but the next verse adds, "But let him ask in faith, nothing doubting: for he that doubteth is like the surge of

he sea driven by the wind and tossed. For let not
hat man think that he shall receive anything of
he Lord." (R. V.) There must then be confident,
inwavering expectation. But there is a faith that
;oes beyond expectation, that believes that the
)rayer is heard and the promise granted. This
:omes out in the Revised Version of Mark 11:24,
'Therefore I say unto you, All things whatsoever
7e pray and ask for, believe that ye *have* received
:hem, and ye shall have them."

But how can one get this faith?

Let us say with all emphasis, it cannot be pumped
ip. Many a one reads this promise about the
)rayer of faith, and then asks for things that he
lesires and tries to make himself believe that God
1as heard the prayer. This ends only in disap-
)ointment, for it is not real faith and the thing
s not granted. It is at this point that many peo-
)le make a collapse of faith altogether by trying
:o work up faith by an effort of their will, and
is the thing they made themselves believe they
:xpected to get is not given, the very foundation
)f faith is oftentimes undermined.

But how does real faith come?

Romans 10:17 answers the question: "So then
:aith cometh by hearing, and hearing *by the Word*
)f *God*." If we are to have real faith, we must

study the Word of God and find out what is promised, then simply believe the promises of God. Faith must have a warrant. Trying to believe something that you want to believe is not faith. Believing what God says in His Word is faith. If I am to have faith when I pray, I must find some promise in the Word of God on which to rest my faith. Faith furthermore comes through the Spirit. The Spirit knows the will of God, and if I pray in the Spirit, and look to the Spirit to teach me God's will, He will lead me out in prayer along the line of that will, and give me faith that the prayer is to be answered; but in no case does real faith come by simply determining that you are going to get the thing that you want to get. If there is no promise in the Word of God, and no clear leading of the Spirit, there can be no real faith, and there should be no upbraiding of self for lack of faith in such a case. But if the thing desired is promised in the Word of God, we may well upbraid ourselves for lack of faith if we doubt; for we are making God a liar by doubting His Word.

Chapter 6

ALWAYS PRAYING AND NOT
FAINTING

N TWO PARABLES in the Gospel of Luke, Jesus teaches with great emphasis the lesson that
en ought always to pray and not to faint. The
st parable is found in Luke 11:5-8, and the
her in Luke 18:1-8.

"And he said unto them, Which of you shall
ve a friend, and shall go unto him at midnight,
d say unto him, Friend, lend me three loaves
r a friend of mine in his journey is come to me,
d I have nothing to set before him; and he from
ithin shall answer and say, Trouble me not:
e door is now shut, and my children are with
e in bed. I cannot rise and give thee. I say
ito you, Though he will not rise and give him
cause he is his friend, yet because of his im-

portunity he will rise and give him as many as h
needeth" (Luke 11:5-8).

"And he spake a parable unto them to this en
that men ought always to pray and not to faint
saying, There was in a city a judge which feared no
God, neither regarded man; and there was a widov
in that city; and she came to him, saying,

"Avenge me of mine adversary.

"And he would not for a while: but afterward
he said within himself: 'Though I fear not God
nor regard man; yet because of this widov
troubleth me, I will avenge her, lest by her con
tinual coming she weary me.

"And the Lord said, Hear what the unjust judg
saith. And shall not God avenge his own elect
which cry day and night unto him, though h
bear long with them? I tell you that he will aveng
them speedily. Nevertheless when the Son of ma:
cometh, shall he find faith on the earth?" (Luk
18:1-8).

In the former of these two parables Jesus set
forth the necessity of importunity in prayer in
startling way. The word rendered *importunit*
means literally *shamelessness,* as if Jesus woul
have us understand that God would have us dra\
nigh to Him with a determination to obtain th
things we seek that will not be put to shame b

ıy seeming refusal or delay on God's part. God
:lights in the holy boldness that will not take *no*
ır an answer. It is an expression of great faith,
ıd nothing pleases God more than faith.

Jesus seemed to put the Syro-Phoenician woman
vay almost with rudeness; but she would not be
ıt away, and Jesus looked upon her shameless
ıportunity with pleasure, and said, "O woman,
·eat is thy faith: be it unto thee even as thou
ilt" (Matt. 15:28). God does not always let us
:t things at our first effort. He would train us
ıd make us strong men by compelling us to work
ırd for the best things. So also He does not al-
ays give us what we ask in answer to the first
·ayer; He would train us and make us strong
en of prayer by compelling us to pray hard for
ıe best things. He makes us *pray through.*

I am glad that this is so. There is no more
essed training in prayer than that that comes
ırough being compelled to ask again and again
ıd again even through a long period of years be-
ıre one obtains that which he seeks from God.
any people call it submission to the will of God
hen God does not grant them their requests at
ıe first or second asking, and they say,

"Well, perhaps it is not God's will."

As a rule this is not submission, but spiritual laziness. We do not call it submission to the will of God when we give up after one or two efforts to obtain things by action; we call it lack of strength of character. When the strong man of action starts out to accomplish a thing, if he does not accomplish it the first or second or one-hundredth time, he keeps hammering away until he does accomplish it; and the strong man of prayer when he starts to pray for a thing keeps on praying until he prays it through, and obtains what he seeks. We should be careful about what we ask from God, but when we do begin to pray for a thing we should never give up praying for it until we get it, or until God makes it very clear and very definite to us that it is not His will to give it.

Some would have us believe that it shows unbelief to pray twice for the same thing, that we ought to "take it" the first time that we ask. Doubtless there are times when we are able through faith in the Word or the leading of the Holy Spirit to *claim* the first time that which we have asked of God; but beyond question there are other times when we must pray again and again and again for the same thing before we get our answer. Those who have gotten beyond praying twice for the same thing have gotten beyond their Master (Matt. 26:44). George Mueller prayed or two men daily for upwards of sixty years. One of these men was converted shortly before his death, I think at the last service that George Mueller held, the other was converted within a year after his death. One of the great needs of the present day is men and women who will not only start out to pray for things but pray on and on and on until they obtain that which they seek from the Lord.

Chapter 7

ABIDING IN CHRIST

"IF YE ABIDE IN ME and my words abide in you, ye shall ask what ye will, and it shall be done unto you" (John 15:7). The whole secret of prayer is found in these words of our Lord. Here is prayer that has unbounded power: "Ask *what ye will,* and it shall be done unto you."

There is a way then of asking and getting precisely what we ask and getting all we ask. Christ gives two conditions of this all-prevailing prayer:

1. The first condition is, "If ye abide in me." What is it to abide in Christ?

Some explanations that have been given of this are so mystical or so profound that to many simple-minded children of God they mean practically nothing at all; but what Jesus meant was really very simple.

He had been comparing Himself to a vine, His

64

isciples to the branches in the vine. Some branch-
; continued in the vine, that is, remained in liv-
ig union with the vine, so that the sap or life of
ie vine constantly flowed into these branches.
'hey had no independent life of their own. Every-
iing in them was simply the outcome of the life
f the vine flowing into them. Their buds, their
:aves, their blossoms, their fruit, were really not
ieirs, but the buds, leaves, blossoms and fruit of
ie vine. Other branches were completely severed
:om the vine, or else the flow of the sap or life
f the vine into them was in some way hindered.
ow for us to abide in Christ is for us to bear
ie same relation to Him that the first sort of
ranches bear to the vine; that is to say, to abide
i Christ is to renounce any independent life of
ur own, to give up trying to think our thoughts,
r form our resolutions, or cultivate our feelings,
id simply and constantly look to Christ to think
is thoughts in us, to form His purposes in us,
) feel His emotions and affections in us. It is
) renounce all life independent of Christ, and
onstantly to look to Him for the inflow of His
fe into us, and the outworking of His life
irough us. When we do this, and in so far as we
o this, our prayers will obtain that which we
ek from God.

This must necessarily be so, for our desires will not be our own desires but Christ's; and our prayers will not in reality be our own prayers, but Christ praying in us. Such prayers will always be in harmony with God's will, and the Father heareth Him always. When our prayers fail it is because they are indeed our prayers. We have conceived the desire and framed the petition of ourselves, instead of looking to Christ to pray through us.

To say that one should be abiding in Christ in all his prayers, looking to Christ to pray through Him rather than praying himself, is simply saying in another way that one should pray "in the Spirit." When we thus abide in Christ, our thoughts are not our own thoughts, but His; our joys are not our own joys, but His; our fruit is not our own fruit, but His; just as the buds, leaves, blossoms and fruit of the branch that abides in the vine are not the buds, leaves, blossoms and fruit of the branch, but of the vine itself whose life is flowing into the branch and manifests itself in these buds, leaves, blossoms and fruit.

To abide in Christ, one must of course already be in Christ through the acceptance of Christ as an atoning Saviour from the guilt of sin, a risen Saviour from the power of sin, and a Lord and

Master over all his life. Being in Christ, all that we have to do to abide (or continue) in Christ is simply to renounce our self-life—utterly renouncing every thought, every purpose, every desire, every affection of our own and just looking day by day and hour by hour for Jesus Christ to form His thoughts, His purposes, His affections, His desires in us. Abiding in Christ is really a very simple matter, though it is a wonderful life of privilege and of power.

2. But there is another condition stated in this verse, though it is really involved in the first: And my words abide in you."

If we are to obtain from God all that we ask from Him, Christ's words must abide or continue in us. We must study His words, fairly devour His words, let them sink into our thought and into our heart, keep them in our memory, obey them constantly in our life, let them shape and mold our daily life and our every act.

This is really the method of abiding in Christ. It is through His words that Jesus imparts Himself to us. The words He speaks unto us, they are spirit and they are life (John 6:63). It is vain to expect power in prayer unless we meditate much upon the words of Christ, and let them sink deep and find a permanent abode in our hearts. There

are many who wonder why they are so powerless
in prayer, but the very simple explanation of it
all is found in their neglect of the words of Christ.
They have not hidden His words in their hearts;
His words do not abide in them.   It is not by seasons of mystical meditation and rapturous ex-
periences that we learn to abide in Christ; it is by
feeding upon His word, His written word as found
in the Bible, and looking to the Holy Spirit to
implant these words in our hearts and to make
them a living thing in our hearts. If we thus let
the words of Christ abide in us, they will stir us
up to prayer. They will be the mold in which our
prayers are shaped, and our prayers will be necessarily along the line of God's will, and will prevail with Him. Prevailing prayer is almost an
impossibility where there is neglect of the study of
the Word of God.

Mere intellectual study of the Word of God is
not enough; there must be meditation upon it.
The Word of God must be revolved over and over
and over in the mind, with a constant looking to
God by His Spirit to make that Word a living
thing in the heart. The prayer that is born of
meditation upon the Word of God is the prayer
that soars upward most easily to God's listening
ear.

George Mueller, one of the mightiest men of
ayer of the present generation, when the hour
r prayer came would begin by reading and medi-
ting upon God's Word until out of the study
 the Word a prayer began to form itself in his
art. Thus God Himself was the real author of
e prayer, and God answered the prayer which
e Himself had inspired.

The Word of God is the instrument through
hich the Holy Spirit works, it is the sword of the
irit in more senses than one; and the one who
uld know the work of the Holy Spirit in any
rection must feed upon the Word. The one
o would pray in the Spirit must meditate much
on the Word, that the Holy Spirit may have
nething through which He can work. The
ly Spirit works His prayers in us through the
ord, and neglect of the Word makes praying in
e Holy Spirit an impossibility. If we would
d the fire of our prayers with the fuel of God's
ord, all our diffculties in prayer would disap-
ar.

Chapter 8

PRAYING WITH THANKSGIVING

THERE ARE TWO WORDS often overlooked in the lesson about prayer which Paul gives us in Philippians 4:6, 7: "In nothing be anxious; but in everything by prayer and supplication with thanksgiving let your requests be made known unto God. And the peace of God, which passeth all understanding, shall guard your hearts and your thoughts in Christ Jesus" (R. V.) The two important words often overlooked are *with thanksgiving*.

In approaching God to ask for new blessings, we should never forget to return thanks for blessings already granted. If any one of us would stop and think how many of the prayers which we have offered to God have been answered, and how seldom we have gone back to God to return thanks for the answers thus given, I am sure we would be overwhelmed with confusion. We should be just as definite in returning thanks as we are in prayer. We come to God with most specific petitions, but when we return thanks to Him our thanksgiving is indefinite and general.

Doubtless one reason why so many of our prayers lack power is because we have neglected to return thanks for blessings already received. If anyone were to constantly come to us asking help from us, and should never say "Thank you" for the help thus given, we would soon tire of helping one so ungrateful. Indeed, regard for the one we were helping would hold us back from encouraging such rank ingratitude. Doubtless our heavenly Father out of a wise regard for our highest welfare oftentimes refuses to answer petitions that we send up to Him in order that we may be brought to a sense of our ingratitude and taught to be thankful.

God is deeply grieved by the thanklessness and ingratitude of which so many of us are guilty. When Jesus healed the ten lepers and only one came back to give Him thanks, in wonderment and pain He exclaimed,

"Were not the ten cleansed? but where are the nine?" (Luke 17:17, R. V.).

How often must He look down upon us in sadness at our forgetfulness of His repeated blessings, and His frequent answer to our prayers.

Returning thanks for blessings already received increases our faith and enables us to approach God with new boldness and new assurance. Doubtless the reason so many have so little faith when they pray is because they take so little time to meditate upon and thank God for blessings already received. As one meditates upon the answers to prayers already granted, faith waxes bolder and bolder, and we come to feel in the very depths of our souls that there is nothing too hard for the Lord. As we reflect upon the wondrous goodness of God toward us on the one hand, and upon the other hand upon the little thought and strength and time that we ever put into thanksgiving, we may well humble ourselves before God and confess our sin.

The mighty men of prayer in the Bible, and the mighty men of prayer throughout the ages of the church's history have been men who were much given to thanksgiving and praise. David was a mighty man of prayer, and now his Psalms abound with thanksgiving and praise. The apostles were mighty men of prayer; of them we read that "they were continually in the temple, praising and blessing God." Paul was a mighty man of prayer, and how often in his epistles he bursts out

n definite thanksgiving to God for definite bless-
ngs and definite answers to prayers. Jesus is our
nodel in prayer as in everything else. We find in
he study of His life that His manner of returning
hanks at the simplest meal was so noticeable that
wo of His disciples recognized Him by this after
His resurrection.

Thanksgiving is one of the inevitable results of
)eing filled with the Holy Spirit and one who
loes not learn "in everything to give thanks" can-
10t continue to pray in the Spirit. If we would
earn to pray with power we would do well to let
hese two words sink deep into our hearts: *"With
hanksgiving."*

Chapter 9

HINDRANCES TO PRAYER

WE HAVE GONE very carefully into the positive conditions of prevailing prayer; but there are some things which hinder prayer. These God has made very plain in His Word.

1. The first hindrance to prayer we will find in James 4:3, "Ye ask and receive not *because ye ask amiss, that ye may spend it in your pleasures*" (R. V.).

A selfish purpose in prayer robs prayer of power. Very many prayers are selfish. These may be prayers for things for which it is perfectly proper to ask, for things which it is the will of God to give, but the motive of the prayer is entirely wrong, and so the prayer falls powerless to the ground. The true purpose in prayer is that God may be glorified in the answer. If we ask

74

any petition merely that we may receive something to use in our pleasures or in our own gratification in one way or another, we "ask amiss" and
need not expect to receive what we ask. This explains why many prayers remain unanswered.

For example, many a woman is praying for the
conversion of her husband. That certainly is a
most proper thing to ask; but many a woman's
motive in asking for the conversion of her husband
is entirely improper, it is selfish. She desires that
her husband may be converted because it would
be so much more pleasant for her to have a husband who sympathized with her; or it is so pain-
ful to think that her husband might die and be
lost forever. For some such selfish reason as this
she desires to have her husband converted. The
prayer is purely selfish. Why should a woman
desire the conversion of her husband? First of
all and above all, that God may be glorified; because she cannot bear the thought that God the
Father should be dishonored by her husband
trampling under foot the Son of God.

Many pray for a revival. That certainly is a
prayer that is pleasing to God; it is along the line
of His will; but many prayers for revivals are purely selfish. The churches desire revivals in order that
the membership may be increased, in order that

the church may have a position of more power
and influence in the community, in order that the
church treasury may be filled, in order that a good
report may be made at the presbytery or confer-
ence or association. For such low purposes as
these, churches and ministers oftentimes are praying for a revival, and oftentimes too God does
not answer the prayer. Why should we pray for
a revival? For the glory of God, because we cannot endure it that God should continue to be dishonored by the worldliness of the church, by the
sins of unbelievers, by the proud unbelief of the
day; because God's Word is being made void; in
order that God may be glorified by the outpouring
of His Spirit on the Church of Christ. For these
reasons first of all and above all, we should pray
for a revival.

Many a prayer for the Holy Spirit is a purely
selfish prayer. It certainly is God's will to give
the Holy Spirit to them that ask Him—He has
told us so plainly in His Word (Luke 11:13), but
many a prayer for the Holy Spirit is hindered by
the selfishness of the motive that lies back of the
prayer. Men and women pray for the Holy Spirit
in order that they may be happy, or in order that
they may be saved from the wretchedness of de-
feat in their lives, or in order that they may have

power as Christian workers, or for some other
purely selfish motive Why should we pray for
the Spirit? In order that God may no longer be
dishonored by the low level of our Christian lives
and by our ineffectiveness in service; in order that
God may be glorified in the new beauty that comes
into our lives and the new power that comes into
our service.

2. The second hindrance to prayer we find in
Isaiah 59:1, 2: "Behold, the Lord's hand is not
shortened, that it cannot save; neither his ear
heavy, that it cannot hear. But *your inquities
have separated between you and your God, and
your sins have hid his face from you, that he will
not hear.*"

Sin hinders prayer. Many a man prays and
prays and prays, and gets absolutely no answer to
his prayer. Perhaps he is tempted to think that
it is not the will of God to answer or he may think
that the days when God answered prayer, if He
ever did, are over. So the Israelites seem to have
thought. They thought that the Lord's hand was
shortened, that it could not save, and that His ear
had become heavy that it could no longer hear.

"Not so," said Isaiah, "God's ear is just as open
to hear as ever, His hand just as mighty to save;
but there is a hindrance. That hindrance is your

own sins. Your iniquities have separated between
you and your God, and your sins have hid His
face from you that He will not hear."

It is so today. Many and many a man is crying to God in vain, simply because of sin in his
life. It may be some sin in the past that has been
unconfessed and unjudged, it may be some sin in
the present that is cherished, very likely is not
even looked upon as sin; but there the sin is, hidden away somewhere in the heart or in the life,
and God "will not hear."

Anyone who finds his prayers ineffective should
not conclude that the thing which he asks of God
is not according to His will, but should go alone
with God with the Psalmist's prayer, "Search me,
O God, and know my heart: try me, and know
my thoughts: and see if there be any wicked way
in me" (Ps. 139:23, 24), and wait before Him
until He puts His finger upon the thing that is
displeasing in His sight. Then this sin should be
confessed and put away.

I well remember a time in my life when I was
praying for two definite things that it seemed that
I must have, or God would be dishonored; but the
answer did not come. I awoke in the middle of
the night in great physical suffering and great distress of soul. I cried to God for these things, rea-

soned with Him as to how necessary it was that I get them, and get them at once; but no answer came. I asked God to show me if there was anything wrong in my own life. Something came to my mind that had often come to it before, something definite but which I was unwilling to confess as sin. I said to God, "If this is wrong I will give it up"; but still no answer came. In my innermost heart, though I had never admitted it, I knew it was wrong.

At last I said:

"This is wrong. I have sinned. I will give it up."

I found peace. In a few moments I was sleeping like a child. In the morning I woke well in body, and the money that was so much needed for the honor of God's name came.

Sin is an awful thing, and one of the most awful things about it is the way it hinders prayer, the way it severs the connection between us and the source of all grace and power and blessing. Anyone who would have power in prayer must be merciless in dealing with his own sins. "If I regard iniquity in my heart, the Lord will not hear me" (Ps. 66:18). So long as we hold on to sin or have any controversy with God, we cannot expect Him to heed our prayers. If there is anything that is constantly coming up in your moments of close communion with God, that is the things that hinders prayer: put it away.

3. The third hindrance to prayer is found in Ezekiel 14:3, "Son of man, these men have taken their idols into their heart, and put the stumbling block of their iniquity before their face: should I be inquired of at all by them?" (R. V.) *Idols in the heart cause God to refuse to listen to our prayers.*

What is an idol?   An idol is anything that takes the place of God, anything that is the supreme object of our affection. God alone has the right to the supreme place in our hearts. Everything and everyone else must be subordinate to Him.

Many a man makes an idol of his wife. Not that a man can love his wife any too much, but he can put her in the wrong place; he can put her before God; and when a man regards his wife's pleasure before God's pleasure, when he gives her the first place and God the second place, his wife is an idol, and God cannot hear his prayers.

Many a woman makes an idol of her children. Not that we can love our children too much. The more dearly we love Christ, the more dearly we love our children; but we can put our children in the wrong place, we can put them before God, and their interests before God's interests. When we do this our children are our idols.

Many a man makes an idol of his reputation or his business. Reputation or business is put before God. God cannot hear the prayers of such a man.

One great question for us to decide, if we would have power in prayer is, Is God absolutely first? Is He before wife, before children, before reputation, before business, before our own lives? If not, prevailing prayer is impossible.

God often calls our attention to the fact that we have an idol by not answering our prayers, and thus leading us to inquire as to why our prayers are not answered; and so we discover the idol, put it away and God hears our prayers.

4. The fourth hindrance to prayer is found in Proverbs 21:13, *"Whoso stoppeth his ears at the cry of the poor,* he also shall cry himself, but shall not be heard."

There is perhaps no greater hindrance to prayer than stinginess, the lack of liberality toward the poor and toward God's work. It is the one who gives generously to others who receives generously from God. "Give, and it shall be given unto you; good measure pressed down, shaken together, running over, shall they give into your bosom. For

with what measure ye mete it shall be measured
to you again" (Luke 6:38, R. V.). The generous
man is the mighty man of prayer. The stingy
man is the powerless man of prayer.

One of the most wonderful statements about
prevailing prayer (already referred to) I John
3:22, "Whatsoever we ask we receive of him, because we keep his commandments, and do those
things that are pleasing in his sight," is made in
direct connection with generosity toward the
needy. In the context we are told that it is when
we love, not in word or in tongue, but in deed
and in truth, when we open our hearts toward the
brother in need, it is then and only then we have
confidence toward God in prayer.

Many a man and woman who is seeking to find
the secret of their powerlessness in prayer need
not seek far; it is nothing more nor less than downright stinginess. George Mueller, to whom refer-
ence has already been made, was a mighty man
of prayer because he was a mighty giver. What
he received from God never stuck to his fingers;
he immediately passed it on to others. He was
constantly receiving because he was constantly giving. When one thinks of the selfishness of the
professing church today, how the orthodox
churches of this land do not average one dollar per

year per member for foreign missions, it is no
wonder that the church has so little power in
prayer. If we would get from God, we must
give to others. Perhaps the most wonderful promise in the Bible in regard to God's supplying our
need is Philippians 4:19, "And my God shall ful-
fill every need of yours according to his riches in
glory in Christ Jesus" (R. V.). This glorious
promise was made to the Philippian church, and
made in immediate connection with their generosity.

5. The fifth hindrance to prayer is found in
Mark 11:25, "And when ye stand praying, *forgive*,
if ye have ought against any; that your Father also which is in heaven may forgive you your trespasses."

An unforgiving spirit is one of the commonest
hindrances to prayer. Prayer is answered on the
basis that our sins are forgiven; but God cannot
deal with us on the basis of forgiveness while we
are harboring ill will against those who have
have wronged us. Anyone who is nursing a grudge
against another has fast closed the ear of God
against his own petition. How many there are
crying to God for the conversion of husband, children, friends, and wondering why it is that their
prayer is not answered, when the whole secret is

some grudge that they have in their hearts against someone who has injured them, or who they fancy has injured them. Many and many a mother and father are allowing their children to go down to eternity unsaved, for the miserable gratification of hating somebody.

6. The sixth hindrance to prayer is found in I Peter 3:7, "Ye husbands, in like manner, dwell with your wives according to knowledge, giving honor unto the woman, as unto the weaker vessel as being also joint-heirs of the grace of life; to the end that your prayers be not hindered" (R. V.). Here we are plainly told that *a wrong relation between husband and wife is a hindrance to prayer.*

In many and many a case the prayers of husbands are hindered because of their failure of duty toward their wives. On the other hand, it is also doubtless true that the prayers of wives are hindered because of their failure in duty toward their husbands. If husbands and wives should seek diligently to find the cause of their unanswered prayers, they would often find it in their relations to one another.

Many a man who makes great pretentions to piety, and is very active in Christian work, shows but little consideration in his treatment of his wife, and is oftentimes unkind, if not brutal; then

e wonders why it is that his prayers are not an-
vered. The verse that we have just quoted ex-
lains the seeming mystery. On the other hand,
any a woman who is very devoted to the church,
nd very faithful in attendance upon all services,
eats her husband with the most unpardonable
eglect, is cross and peevish toward him, wounds
im by the sharpness of her speech, and by her
ngovernable temper; then wonders why it is that
ie has no power in prayer.

There are other things in the relations of hus-
ands and wives which cannot be spoken of pub-
cly, but which doubtless are oftentimes a hin-
rance in approaching God in prayer. There is
uch of sin covered up under the holy name of
arriage that is a cause of spiritual deadness, and
f powerlessness in prayer. Any man or woman
hose prayers seems to bring no answer should
iread their whole married life out before God,
id ask Him to put His finger upon anything in
that is displeasing in His sight.

7. The seventh hindrance to prayer is found
i James 1:5-7, "But if any of you lacketh wis-
om, let him ask of God, who giveth to all liberal-
· and upbraideth not; and it shall be given him.
ut let him ask *in faith, nothing doubting:* for he
iat doubteth is like the surge of the sea driven by

the wind and tossed. For let not that man think that he shall receive anything of the Lord" (R. V.).

Prayers are hindered by unbelief. God demands that we shall believe His Word absolutely. To question it is to make Him a liar. Many of us do that when we plead His promises, and is it any wonder that our prayers are not answered? How many prayers are hindered by our wretched unbelief! We go to God and ask Him for something that is positively promised in His Word, and then we do not more than half expect to get it. "Let not that man think that he shall receive anything of the Lord."

Chapter 10

WHEN TO PRAY

IF WE WOULD KNOW the fullness of blessing that there is in the prayer life, it is important not only that we pray in the right way, but also that we pray at the right time. Christ's own example is full of suggestiveness as to the right time for prayer.

1. In the first chapter of Mark, verse 35, we read, "And *in the morning,* rising up *a great while before day,* he went out, and departed into a solitary place, and there prayed."

Jesus chose the early morning hour for prayer. Many of the mightiest men of God have followed the Lord's example in this. In the morning hour the mind is fresh and at its very best. It is free from distraction, and that absolute concentration upon God which is essential to the most effective

87

prayer is most easily possible in the early morning hours. Furthermore, when the early hours are spent in prayer the whole day is sanctified, and power is obtained for overcoming its temptations, and for performing its duties. More can be accomplished in prayer in the first hours of the day than at any other time during the day. Every child of God who would make the most out of his life for Christ should set apart the first part of the day to meeting God in the study of His Word and in prayer. The first thing we do each day should be to go alone with God and face the duties, the temptations, and the service of that day, and get strength from God for all. We should get victory before the hour of trial, temptation, or service comes. The secret place of prayer is the place to fight our battles and gain our victories.

2. In the sixth chapter of Luke, verse 12, we get further light upon the right time to pray. We read, "And it came to pass in those days, and he went out into a mountain to pray, and continued *all night* in prayer to God."

Here we see Jesus praying in the night, spending the entire night in prayer. Of course we have no reason to suppose that this was the constant practice of our Lord, nor do we even know how com-

non this practice was, but there were certainly
imes when the whole night was given up to
>rayer. Here too we do well to follow in the foot-
teps of the Master.

Of course there is a way of setting apart nights
or prayer in which there is no profit; it is pure
egalism. But the abuse of this practice is no rea-
on for neglecting it altogether. One ought not
:o say, "I am going to spend a whole night in
>rayer," with the thought that there is any merit
:hat will win God's favor in such an exercise; that
s legalism. But we oftentimes do well to say, "I
im going to set apart this night for meeting God,
ind obtaining His blessing and power; and if neces-
ary, and if He so leads me, I will give the whole
night to prayer." Oftentimes we will have prayed
:hings through long before the night has passed,
ind we can retire and find more refreshing and
nvigorating sleep than if we had not spent the
:ime in prayer. At other times God doubtless will
ceep us in communion with Himself away into
:he morning; and when He does this in His infinite
grace, blessed indeed are these hours of night
>rayer!

Nights of prayer to God are followed by days
>f power with men. In the night hours the world
s hushed in slumber, and we can easily be alone

with God and have undisturbed communion with Him. If we set apart the whole night for prayer, there will be no hurry, there will be time for our own hearts to become quiet before God, there will be time for the whole mind to be brought under the guidance of the Holy Spirit, there will be plenty of time to pray things through. A night of prayer should be put entirely under God's control. We should lay down no rules as to how long we will pray, or as to what we shall pray about, but be ready to wait upon God for a short time or a long time as He may lead, and to be led out in one direction or another as He may see fit.

3. Jesus Christ prayed *before all the great crises in His earthly life.*

He prayed before choosing the twelve disciples; before the sermon on the mount; before starting out on an evangelistic tour; before His anointing with the Holy Spirit and His entrance upon His public ministry; before announcing to the Twelve His approaching death; before the great consummation of His life at the cross (Luke 6:12, 13; Luke 9:18, 21, 22; Luke 3:21, 22; Mark 1:35-38; Luke 32:39-46). He prepared for every important crisis by a protracted season of prayer. So ought we to do also. Whenever any crisis of life is seen to be approaching, we should prepare

for it by a season of very definite prayer to God.
We should take plenty of time for this prayer.

4.   Christ prayed not only before the great
events and victories of His life, but He also prayed
after its great achievements and important crises.

When He had fed the five thousand with the
five loaves and two fishes, and the multitude desired to take Him and make Him king, having
sent them away He went up into the mountain
apart to pray, and spent hours there alone in prayer
to God (Matt. 14:23; John 6:15). So He went
on from victory to victory.

It is more common for most of us to pray before the great events of life than it is to pray
after them, but the latter is as important as
the former. If we would pray after the
great achievements of life, we might go on
to still greater; as it is we are often either
puffed up or exhausted by the things that we do in
the name of the Lord, and so we advance no
further. Many and many a man in answer to
prayer has been endued with power and thus has
wrought great things in the name of the Lord,
and when these great things were accomplished,
instead of going alone with God and humbling
himself before Him, and giving Him all the glory
for what was achieved, he has congratulated him-

self upon what has been accomplished, has become
puffed up, and God has been obliged to lay him
aside. The great things done were not followed by
humiliation of self, and prayer to God, and so
pride has come in and the mighty man has been
shorn of his power.

5. Jesus Christ gave a special time to prayer
when life was unusually busy. He would withdraw in such a time from the multitudes that
thronged about Him, and go into the wilderness
and pray. For example, we read in Luke 5:15, 16,
"But so much the more went abroad the report
concerning him and great multitudes came to
gether to hear, and to be healed of their infirmi-
ties. But he withdrew himself in the deserts and
prayed" (R. V.).

Some men are so busy that they find no time
for prayer. Apparently the busier Christ's life
was, the more He prayed. Sometimes He had no
time to eat (Mark 3:20), sometimes He had no
time for needed rest and sleep (Mark 6:31, 33,
46); but He always took time to pray; and the
more the work crowded the more He prayed.

Many a mighty man of God has learned this
secret from Christ, and when the work has crowded more than usual they have set an unusual
amount of time apart for prayer. Other men of

God, once mighty, have lost their power because they did not learn this secret, and allowed increasing work to crowd out prayer.

Years ago it was the writer's privilege, with other theological students, to ask questions of one of the most useful Christian men of the day. The writer was led to ask,

"Will you tell us something of your prayer life?"

The man was silent a moment, and then, turning his eyes earnestly upon me, replied:

"Well, I must admit that I have been so crowded with work of late that I have not given the time I should to prayer."

Is it any wonder that that man lost power, and the great work that he was doing was curtailed in a very marked degree? Let us never forget that the more the work presses on us, the more time must we spend in prayer.

6. Jesus Christ prayed *before the great temptations of His life.*

As He drew nearer and nearer to the cross, and realized that upon it was to come the great final test of His life, Jesus went out into the garden to pray. He came "unto a place called Gethsemane, and saith unto the disciples, Sit ye here while I go and pray yonder" (Matt. 26:36). The victory of Calvary was won that night in the garden of Gethsemane. The calm majesty of His bearing in meeting the awful onslaughts of Pilate's Judgment Hall and of Calvary, was the outcome of the struggle, agony and victory of Gethsemane. While Jesus prayed the disciples slept, so He stood fast while they fell ignominiously.

Many temptations come upon us unawares and unannounced, and all that we can do is to lift a cry to God for help then and there; but many of the temptations of life we can see approaching from the distance, and in such cases the victory should be won before the temptation really reaches us.

7. In I Thessalonians 5:17 we read, "Pray *without ceasing*," and in Ephesians 6:18 (R. V.), "Praying *at all seasons*."

Our whole life should be a life of prayer. We should walk in constant communion with God. There should be a constant upward looking of the soul to God. We should walk so habitually in His presence that even when we awake in the night it would be the most natural thing in the world for us to speak to Him in thanksgiving or in petition.

Chapter 11

THE NEED OF A GENERAL REVIVAL

IF WE ARE TO PRAY ARIGHT in such a time as this, much of our prayer should be for a general revival. If there was ever a time in which there was need to cry unto God in the words of the Psalmist, "Wilt thou not revive us again, that thy people may rejoice in thee?" (Ps. 85:6), it is this day in which we live. It is surely time for the Lord to work, for men have made void His law (Ps. 119:126). The voice of the Lord given in the written Word is set at naught both by the world and the church. Such a time is not a time for discouragement—the man who believes in God and believes in the Bible can never be discouraged; but it is a time for Jehovah Himself to step in and work. The intelligent Christian, the wide-awake watchman on the walls of

Zion, may well cry with the Psalmist of old, "It is time for Jehovah to work, for they have made void thy law" (Ps. 119:126, R. V.).

The great need of the day is a general revival. Let us consider first of all what a general re-vival is.

A revival is a time of quickening or impartation of life. As God alone can give life, a revival is a time when God visits His people and by the power of His Spirit imparts new life to them, and through them imparts life to sinners dead in trespasses and sins. We have religious excitements gotten up by the cunning methods and hypnotic influence of the mere professional evangelist; but these are not revivals and are not needed. They are the devil's imitations of a revival. *New life from God—* that is a revival. A general revival is a time when this new life from God is not confined to scattered localities, but is general throughout Christendom and the earth.

The reason why a general revival is needed is that spiritual dearth and desolation and death is general. It is not confined to any one country, though it may be more manifest in some countries than in others. It is found in foreign mission fields as well as in home fields. We have had local revivals. The lifegiving Spirit of God has

reathed upon this minister and that, this church
nd that, this community and that; but we need,
ve sorely need, a revival that shall be widespread
nd general.

Let us look for a few moments at the results of
ι revival. These results are apparent in minis-
ers of the church and in the unsaved.

1.   The results of a revival in a minister are

a) The minister has a new love for souls. We
ninisters as a rule have no such love for souls as
ve ought to have, no such love for souls as Jesus
ιad, no such love for souls as Paul had. But when
God visits His people, the heart of ministers are
greatly burdened for the unsaved. They go out
n great longing for the salvation of their fellow
nen. They forget their ambition to preach great
ermons and for fame, and simply long to see men
rought to Christ.

b) When true revivals come, ministers get a
ιew love for God's Word and a new faith in God's
Word. They fling to the winds their doubts and
criticisms of the Bible and of the creeds, and go
to preaching the Bible and especially Christ cruci-
fied. Revivals make ministers who are loose in
their doctrines orthodox. A genuine, wide-sweep-
ing revival would do more to turn things upside

down and thus get them right side up than all the heresy trials ever instituted.

c) Revivals bring to ministers new liberty and power in preaching. It is no week-long grind to prepare a sermon, and no nerve-consuming effort to preach it after it has been prepared. Preaching is a joy and a refreshment, and there is power in it in times of revival.

2. The results of a revival on Christians generally are as marked as its results upon the ministry.

a) In times of revival Christians come out from the world and live separated lives. Christians who have been dallying with the world, who have been playing cards and dancing and going to the theater and indulging in similar follies, give them up. These things are found to be incompatible with increasing life and light.

b) In times of revival Christians get a new spirit of prayer. Prayer meetings are no longer a duty, but become the necessity of a hungry, importunate heart. Private prayer is followed with new zest. The voice of earnest prayer to God is heard day and night. People no longer ask, "Does God answer prayer?" They know He does, and besiege the throne of grace day and night.

c) In times of revival Christians go to work for

t souls. They do not go to meeting simply to
joy themselves and get blessed. They go to
:eting to watch for souls and to bring them to
irist. They talk to men on the street and in the
ires and in their homes. The cross of Christ,
vation, Heaven and Hell become the subjects of
nstant conversation. Politics and the weather
d new bonnets and the latest novels are for-
tten.

d) In times of revival Christians have new joy
Christ. Life is joy, and new life is new joy.
·vival days are glad days, days of Heaven on
:th.

e) In times of revival Christians get a new love
r the Word of God. They want to study it day
d night. Revivals are bad for saloons and theaters,
t they are good for bookstores and Bible agen-
:s.

3. But revivals also have a decided influence
the unsaved world.

a) First of all, they bring deep conviction of
. Jesus said that when the Spirit was come He
)uld convince the world of sin (John 16:7, 8).
)w we have seen that a revival is a coming of
₂ Holy Spirit, and therefore there must be new
nviction of sin, and there always is. If you see
nething men call a revival, and there is no con-

viction of sin, you may know at once that it i
bogus. It is a sure mark.

b) Revivals bring also conversion and regenera·
tion. When God refreshes His people, He alway.
converts sinners also. The first result of Pentecos·
was new life and power to the one hundred anc
twenty disciples in the upper room; the secon(
result was three thousand conversions in a singl(
day. It is always so. I am constantly reading o:
revivals here and there, where Christians wer(
greatly helped but there were no conversions. :
have my doubts about that kind. If Christians ar(
truly refreshed, they will get after the unsaved b^
prayer and testimony and persuasion, and ther(
will be conversions.

Why General Revival Is Needed

We see what a general revival is, and what i
does; let us now face the question why it is needec
at the present time.

I think that the mere description of what it i
and what it does shows that it is needed, sorel^
needed, but let us look at some specific condition
that exist today that show the need of it. In show
ing these conditions one is likely to be called
pessimist. If facing the facts is to be called
pessimist, I am willing to be called a pessimist. I
in order to be an optimist one must shut his eye

nd call black white, and error truth, and sin
ghteousness, and death life, I don't want to be
alled an optimist. But I am an optimist all the
ime. Pointing out the real condition will lead
) a better condition.

1. Look first at the ministry.

a) Many of us who are professedly orthodox
ninisters are practically infidels. That is plain
)eech, but it is also indisputable fact. There is no
ssential difference between the teachings of Tom
'aine and Bob Ingersoll and the teachings of some
f our theological professors. The latter are not
) blunt and honest about it; they phrase it in
nore elegant and studied sentences; but it means
he same. Much of the so-called new learning and
igher criticism is simply Tom Paine infidelity
ugar-coated. Professor Howard Osgood, who is
real scholar and not a mere echo of German in-
idelity, once read a statement of some positions,
nd asked if they did not fairly represent the
cholarly criticism of today; and when it was
greed that they did, he startled his audience by
aying:

"I am reading from Tom Paine's *Age of Rea-*
on."

There is little new in the higher criticism. Our
'uture ministers oftentimes are being educated un-

der infidel professors, and being immature boys
when they enter the college or seminary, they
naturally come out infidels in many cases, and then
go forth to poison the church.

b) Even when our ministers are orthodox—as
thank God, so very many are—they are oftentimes
not men of prayer. How many modern ministers
know what it is to wrestle in prayer, to spend a
good share of a night in prayer? I do not know
how many, but I do know that many do not.

c) Many of us who are ministers have no love
for souls. How many preach because they *must*
preach, because they feel that men everywhere
are perishing, and by preaching they hope to save
some? And how many follow up their preaching
as Paul did, by beseeching men everywhere to be
reconciled to God?

Perhaps enough has been said about us ministers
but it is evident that a revival is needed for our
sake, or some of us will have to stand before God
overwhelmed with confusion in an awful day of
reckoning that is surely coming.

2. Look now at the church:

a) Look at the doctrinal state of the church. It
is bad enough. Many do not believe in the whole
Bible. The book of Genesis is a myth, Jonah is an
allegory, and even the miracles of the Son of God

are questioned. The doctrine of prayer is old-fashioned, and the work of the Holy Spirit is sneered at. Conversion is unnecessary, and Hell is no longer believed in. Then look at the fads and errors that have sprung up out of this loss of faith, Christian Science, Unitarianism, Spiritualism, Universalism, Babism, Metaphysical Healing, etc., etc., a perfect pandemonium of doctrines of devils.

b) Look at the spiritual state of the church. Worldliness is rampant among church members. Many church members are just as eager as any in the rush to get rich. They use the methods of the world in the accumulation of wealth, and they hold just as fast to it as any when they have gotten it.

Prayerlessness abounds among church members on every hand. Someone has said that Christians on the average do not spend more than five minutes a day in prayer.

Neglect of the Word of God goes hand in hand with neglect of prayer to God. Very many Christians spend twice as much time every day wallowing through the mire of the daily papers as they do bathing in the cleansing laver of God's Holy Word. How many Christians average an hour a day spent in Bible study?

Along with neglect of prayer and neglect of the Word of God goes a lack of generosity. The churches are rapidly increasing in wealth, but the treasuries of the missionary societies are empty. Christians do not average a dollar a year for foreign missions. It is simply appalling.

Then there is the increasing disregard for the Lord's Day. It is fast becoming a day of worldly pleasure, instead of a day of holy service. The Sunday newspaper with its inane twaddle and filthy scandal takes the place of the Bible; and visiting and golf and bicycle, the place of the Sunday school and church service.

Christians mingle with the world in all forms of questionable amusements. The young man or young woman who does not believe in dancing with its rank immodesties, in the card table with its drift toward gambling, and in the theater with its ever increasing appeal to lewdness, is counted an old fogey.

Then how small a proportion of our membership has really entered into fellowship with Jesus Christ in His burden for souls! Enough has been said of the spiritual state of the church.

3. Now look at the state of the world.

a) Note how few conversions there are. The Methodist church, which has led the way in ag-

gressive was has actually lost more members than
it has gained the last year. Here and there a church
has a large number of accessions upon confession
of faith, but these churches are rare exceptions;
and where there are such accessions, in how few
cases are the conversions deep, thorough and sat-
isfactory.

b) There is lack of conviction of sin. Seldom
are men overwhelmed with a sense of their awful
guilt in trampling under foot the Son of God. Sin
is regarded as a "misfortune" or as "infirmity,"
or even as "good in the making"; seldom as
enormous wrong against a holy God.

c) Unbelief is rampant. Many regard it as a
mark of intellectual superiority to reject the Bible, and even faith in God and immortality. It is
about the only mark of intellectual superiority
many possess, and perhaps that is the reason they
cling to it so tenaciously.

d) Hand in hand with this widespread infidelity
goes gross immorality, as has always been the case.
Infidelity and immorality are Siamese twins. They
always exist and always grow and always fatten
together. This prevailing immorality is found
everywhere.

Look at the legalized adultery that we call di-
vorce. Men marry one wife after another, and

are still admitted into good society; and women do likewise. There are thousands of supposedly respectable men in America living with other men's wives, and thousands of supposedly respectable women living with other women's husbands.

This immorality is found in the theater. The theater at its best is bad enough, but now the "Sapphos," and the "Degenerates," and all the unspeakable vile accessories of the stage rule the day, and the women who debauch themselves by appearing in such plays are defended in the newspapers and welcomed by supposedly respectable people.

Much of our literature is rotten, but decent people will read books as bad as *Trilby* because it is the rage. Art is oftentimes a mere covering for shameless indecency. Women are induced to cast modesty to the winds that the artist may perfect his art and defile his morals.

Greed for money has become a mania with rich and poor. The multimillionaire will often sell his soul and trample the rights of his fellow men under foot in the mad hope of becoming a billionaire, and the laboring man will often commit murder to increase the power of the union and keep up wages. Wars are waged and men shot down like dogs to improve commerce, and to gain political prestige for unprincipled politicians who parade as statesmen.

The licentiousness of the day lifts its serpent head everywhere. You see it in the newspapers, you see it on the billboards, you see it on the advertisements of cigars, shoes, bicycles, patent medicines, corsets and everything else. You see it on the streets at night. You see it just outside the church door. You find it not only in the awful cesspools set apart for it in the great cities, but it is crowding further and further up our business streets and into the residence portions of our cities. Alas! now and then you find it, if you look sharp, in supposedly respectable homes; indeed it will be borne to your ears by the confessions of broken-hearted men and women. The moral condition of the world in our day is disgusting, sickening, appalling.

We need a revival, deep, widespread, general, in the power of the Holy Ghost. It is either a general revival or the dissolution of the church, of the home, of the state. A revival, new life from God, is the cure, and the only cure. That will stem the awful tide of immorality and unbelief. Mere argument will not do it; but a wind from Heaven, a new outpouring of the Holy Ghost, a true God-sent revival will. Infidelity, higher crit-

icism, Christian Science, Spiritualism, Universalism, all will go down before the outpouring of the
Spirit of God. It was not discussion but the
breath of God that relegated Tom Paine, Voltaire,
Volney and other of the old infidels to the limbo
of forgetfulness; and we need a new breath from
God to send the Wellhausens and the Kuenens and
the Grafs and the parrots they have trained to
occupy chairs and pulpits in England and America
to keep them company. I believe that breath from
God is coming.

The great need of today is a general revival. The
need is clear. It admits of no honest difference of
opinion. What then shall we do? Pray. Take up
the Psalmist's prayer, "Revive us again, that thy
people may rejoice in thee." Take up Ezekiel's
prayer, "Come from the four winds, O breath
[breath of God], and breathe upon these slain
that they may live." Hark, I hear a noise! Behold a shaking! I can almost feel the breeze upon my cheek. I can almost see the great living
army rising to their feet. Shall we not pray and
pray and pray and pray, till the Spirit comes and
God revives His people?

Chapter 12

THE PLACE OF PRAYER BEFORE AND DURING REVIVALS

NO TREATMENT of the subject How to Pray would be at all complete if it did not consider the place of prayer in revivals.

The first great revival of Christian history had its origin on the human side in a ten-day prayer meeting. We read of that handful of disciples, "These all with one accord continued steadfastly in prayer" (Acts 1:14, R. V.). The result of that prayer meeting we read of in the second chapter of the Acts of the Apostles, "They were all filled with the Holy Ghost, and began to speak with other tongues, as the Spirit gave them utterance" (v. 4.). Further on in the chapter we read that "there were added unto them in that day about three thousand souls" (v. 41, R. V.). This revival proved genuine and permanent. The converts "continued steadfastly in the apostles' teaching and fellowship, in the breaking of bread and the prayers" (v. 42, R. V.). "And the Lord added to them day by day those that were being saved" (v. 47, R. V.).

Every true revival from that day to this has had its earthly origin in prayer. The great revival under Jonathan Edwards in the eighteenth century began with his famous call to prayer. The marvelous work of grace among the Indians under Brainerd had its origin in the days and nights that Brainerd spent before God in prayer for an enduement of power from on high for this work.

A most remarkable and widespread display of God's reviving power was that which broke out at Rochester, New York, in 1830, under the labors of Charles G. Finney. It not only spread throughout the state but ultimately to Great Britian as well. Mr. Finney himself attributed the power of this work to the spirit of prayer that prevailed. He describes it in his autobiography in the following words:

"When I was on my way to Rochester, as we passed through a village, some thirty miles east of Rochester, a brother minister whom I knew, seeing me on the canal-boat, jumped aboard to have a little conversation with me, intending to ride but a little way and return. He, however, became interested in conversation, and upon finding where I was going, he made up his mind to keep on and go with me to Rochester. We had been there but a few days when this minister became so convicted that he could not help weeping aloud at one time as we passed along the street. The Lord gave him a powerful spirit of prayer, and his heart was broken. As he and I prayed together, I was struck with his faith in regard to what the Lord was going to do there. I recollect he would say, 'Lord, I do not know how it is; but I seem to know that Thou art going to do a great work in this city.' The spirit of prayer was poured out powerfully, so much so that some persons stayed away from the public services to pray, being unable to restrain their feelings under preaching.

"And here I must introduce the name of a man, whom I shall have occasion to mention frequently, Mr. Abel Clary. He was the son of a very excellent man, and an elder of the church where I was converted. He was converted in the same revival in which I was. He had been licensed to preach; but his spirit of prayer was such, he was so burdened with the souls of men, that he was not able to preach much, his whole time and strength being given to prayer. The burden of his soul would frequently be so great that he was unable to stand, and he would writhe and groan in agony. I was well acquainted with him, and knew something of the wonderful spirit of prayer that was upon him. He was a very silent man, as almost all are who have that powerful spirit of prayer.

"The first I knew of his being in Rochester, a gentleman who lived about a mile west of the city, called on me one day and asked me if I knew a Mr. Abel Clary, a minister. I told him that I knew him well.

" 'Well,' he said, 'he is at my house, and has been there for some time, and I don't know what to think of him.'

"I said, 'I have not seen him at any of our meetings.'

'No,' he replied, 'he cannot go to meetings, he says. He prays nearly all the time, day and night, and in such agony of mind that I do not know what to make of it. Sometimes he cannot even stand on his knees, but will lie prostrate on the floor, and groan and pray in a manner that quite astonishes me.'

"I said to the brother, 'I understand it: please keep still. It will all come out right; he will surely prevail.'

"I knew at the time a considerable number of men who were exercised in the same way. A Deacon P——, of Camden, Oneida county; a Deacon T——, of Rodman, Jefferson county; a Deacon B——, of Adams, in the same county; this Mr. Clary and many others among the men, and a large number of women partook of the same spirit, and spent a great part of their time in prayer. Father Nash, as we called him who in several of my fields of labor came to me and aided me, was another of those men that had such a powerful spirit of prevailing prayer. This Mr. Clary continued in Rochester as long as I did, and did not leave it until after I had left. He never, that I could learn, appeared in public, but gave himself wholly to prayer.

"I think it was the second Sabbath that I was at Auburn at this time, I observed in the congregation the solemn face of Mr. Clary. He looked as if he was borne down with an agony of prayer. Being well acquainted with him, and knowing the great gift of God that was upon him, the spirit of prayer, I was very glad to see him there. He sat in the pew with his brother, the doctor, who was also a professor of religion, but who had nothing by experience, I should think, of his brother Abel's great power with God.

"At intermission, as soon as I came down from the pulpit, Mr. Clary, with his brother, met me at the pulpit stairs, and the doctor invited me to go home with him and spend the intermission and get some refreshments. I did so.

"After arriving at his house we were soon summoned to the dinner table. We gathered about the table, and Dr. Clary turned to his brother and said, 'Brother Abel, will you ask the blessing?' Brother Abel bowed his head and began, audibly, to ask a blessing. He had uttered but a sentence or two when he broke instantly down, moved suddenly back from the table, and fled to his chamber. The doctor supposed he had been taken suddenly ill, and rose up and followed him. In a few moments he came down and said, 'Mr. Finney, Brother Abel wants to see you.'

"Said I, 'What ails him?'

"Said he, 'I do not know but he says you know. He appears in great distress, but I think it is the state of his mind.'

"I understood it in a moment, and went to his room. He lay groaning upon the bed, the Spirit making intercession for him, and in him, with groanings that could not be uttered. I had barely entered the room, when he made out to say, 'Pray, Brother Finney.' I knelt down and helped him

n prayer, by leading his soul out for the conver-
ion of sinners. I continued to pray until his dis-
ress passed away, and then I returned to the din-
ier table.

"I understood that this was the voice of God. I
aw the spirit of prayer was upon him, and I felt
iis influence upon myself, and took it for granted
hat the work would move on powerfully. It did
o. The pastor told me afterward that he found
hat in the six weeks that I was there, five hun-
lreds souls had been converted."

Mr. Finney in his lectures on revivals tells of
)ther remarkable awakenings in answer to the
)rayers of God's people. He says in one place,
'A clergyman in W——n told me of a revival
imong his people, which commenced with a zeal-
)us and devoted woman in the church. She be-
:ame anxious about sinners, and went to praying
:or them; she prayed, and her distress increased;
ind she finally came to her minister, and talked
with him, and asked him to appoint an anxious
meeting, for she felt that one was needed. The
minister put her off, for he felt nothing of it.
The next week she came again, and besought him
:o appoint an anxious meeting; she knew there
would be somebody to come, for she felt as if God
was going to pour out His Spirit. He put her off

again. And finally she said to him, 'If you do not appoint an anxious meeting I shall die, for there is certainly going to be a revival.' The next Sabbath he appointed a meeting, and said that if there were any who wished to converse with him about the salvation of their souls, he would meet them on such an evening. He did not know of one, but when he went to the place, to his astonishment he found a large number of anxious inquirers."

In still another place he says, "The first ray of light that broke in upon the midnight which rested on the churches in Oneida county, in the fall of 1825, was from a woman in feeble health, who, I believe had never been in a powerful revival. Her soul was exercised about sinners. She was in agony for the land. She did not know what ailed her, but she kept praying more and more, till it seemed as if her agony would destroy her body. At length she became full of joy and exclaimed, 'God has come! God has come! There is no mistake about it, the work is begun, and is going over all the region!' And sure enough, the work began, and her family were almost all converted, and the work spread all over that part of the country."

The great revival of 1857 in the United States began in prayer and was carried on by prayer

more than by anything else. Dr. Cuyler in an arti-
cle in a religious newspaper some years ago said,
"Most revivals have humble beginnings, and the
fire starts in a few warm hearts. Never despise
the day of small things. During all my own long
ministry, nearly every work of grace has a similar
beginning. One commenced in a meeting gathered at a few hours' notice in a private house. Another commenced in a group gathered for Bible
study by Mr. Moody in our mission chapel. Still
another—the most powerful of all—was kindled
on a bitter January evening at a meeting of young
Christians under my roof. Dr. Spencer, in his
Pastor's Sketches, (the most suggestive book of
its kind I have ever read), tells us that a remarkable revival in his church sprang from the fervent
prayers of a godly old man who was confined to
his room by lameness. That profound Christian,
Dr. Thomas H. Skinner, of the Union Theological
Seminary, once gave me an account of a remarkable coming together of three earnest men in his
study when he was the pastor of the Arch Street
Church in Philadelphia. They literally wrestled
in prayer. They made a clean breast in confession
of sin, and humbled themselves before God. One
and another church officer came in and joined
them. The Heaven-kindled flame soon spread

through the whole congregation in one of the most powerful revivals ever known in that city."

In the early part of the sixteenth century there was a great religious awakening in Ulster, Ireland. The lands of the rebel chiefs which had been forfeited to the British crown, were settled up by a class of colonists who for the most part were governed by a spirit of wild adventure. Real piety was rare. Seven ministers, five from Scotland and two from England, settled in that country, the earliest arrivals being in 1613. Of one of these ministers named Blair it is recorded by a contemporary, "He spent many days and nights in prayer, alone and with others, and was vouchsafed great intimacy with God." Mr. James Glendenning, a man of very meager natural gifts, was a man similarly minded as regards prayer. The work began under this man Glendenning. The historian of the time says, "He was a man who never would have been chosen by a wise assembly of ministers, nor sent to begin a reformation in this land. Yet this was the Lord's choice to begin with him the admirable work of God which I mention on purpose that all may see how the glory is only the Lord's in making a holy nation in this profane land, and that it was 'not by might, nor by power, nor by man's wisdom, but by my Spirit, saith the

Lord.' " In his preaching at Oldstone, multitudes of hearers felt in great anxiety and terror of conscience. They looked on themselves as altogether lost and damned, and cried out, "Men and brethren, what shall we do to be saved?" They were stricken into a swoon by the power of His Word. A dozen in one day were carried out of doors as dead. These were not women, but some of the boldest spirits of the neighborhood; "some who had formerly feared not with their swords to put a whole market town into a fray." Concerning one of them, the historian writes, "I have heard one of them, then a mighty strong man, now a mighty Christian, say that his end in coming into church was to consult with his companions how to work some mischief."

This work spread throughout the whole country. By the year 1626 a monthly concert of prayer was held in Antrim. The work spread beyond the bounds of Down and Antrim to the churches of the neighboring counties. So great became the religious interest that Christians would come thirty or forty miles to the communions, and continue from the time they came till they returned without wearying or making use of sleep. Many of them neither ate nor drank, and yet some of them professed that they "went away most fresh and vigorous, their souls so filled with the sense of God."

This revival changed the whole character of northern Ireland.

Another great awakening in Ireland in 1859 had a somewhat similar origin. By many who did not know, it was thought that this marvelous work came without warning and preparation; but Rev. William Gibson, the moderator of the General Assembly of the Presbyterian Church in Ireland in 1860, in his very interesting and valuable history of the work, tells how there had been preparation for two years. There had been constant discussion in the General Assembly of the low estate of religion, and of the need of a revival. There had been special sessions for prayer. Finally four young men, who became leaders in the origin of the great work, began to meet together in an old schoolhouse in the neighborhood of Kells. About the spring of 1858 a work of power began to manifest itself. It spread from town to town, and from county to county. The congregations became too large for the buildings, and the meetings were held in the open air, oftentimes attended by many thousands of people. Many hundreds of persons were frequently convicted of sin in a single meeting. In some places the criminal courts and ails were closed for lack of occupation. There were manifestations of the Holy Spirit's power of a most remarkable character, clearly proving that the Holy Spirit is as ready to work today as in apostolic days, when ministers and Christians really believe in Him and begin to prepare the way by prayer.

Mr. Moody's wonderful work in England and Scotland and Ireland, that afterwards spread to America, had its origin on the manward side in prayer. Mr. Moody made little impression until men and women began to cry to God. Indeed his going to England at all was in answer to the importunate cries to God of a bed-ridden saint. While the spirit of prayer continued the revival abode in strength, but in the course of time less and less was made of prayer and the work fell off very perceptibly in power. Doubtless one of the great secrets of the unsatisfactoriness and superficiality and unreality of many of our modern so-called revivals is that more dependence is put upon man's machinery than upon God's power, sought and obtained by earnest, persistent, believing prayer. We live in a day characterized by the multiplication of man's machinery and the diminution of God's power. The great cry of our day is work, work, work, new organizations, new

methods, new machinery; the great need of our
day is prayer. It was a master stroke of the Devil
when he got the church so generally to lay aside
this mighty weapon of prayer. The Devil is perfectly willing that the church should multiply
its organizations, and deftly contrive machinery
for the conquest of the world for Christ if it will
only give up praying. He laughs as he looks at
the church today and says to himself,

"You can have your Sunday schools and your
Young People's Societies, your Young Men's Christian Associations and your Women's Christian
Temperance Unions, your Institutional Churches
and your Industrial Schools, and your Boys' Bri-
gades, your grand choirs and your fine organs,
your brilliant preachers and your revival efforts
too, if you don't bring the power of Almighty God
into them by earnest, persistent, believing, mighty
prayer."

Prayer could work as marvelous results today as
it ever could, if the church would only betake itself to it.

There seems to be increasing signs that the
church is awaking to this fact. Here and there
God is laying upon individual ministers and
churches a burden of prayer that they have never
known before. Less dependence is being put upon

machinery and more dependence upon God. Ministers are crying to God day and night for power. Churches and portions of churches are meeting together in the early morning hours and the late night hours crying to God for the latter rain. There is every indication of the coming of a mighty and widespread revival. There is every reason why, if a revival should come in any country at this time, it should be more widespread in its extent than any revival of history. There is the closest and swiftest communication by travel, by letter, and by cable between all parts of the world. A true fire of God kindled in America would soon spread to the uttermost parts of the earth. The only thing needed to bring this fire is prayer.

It is not necessary that the whole church get to praying to begin with. Great revivals always begin first in the hearts of a few men and women whom God arouses by His Spirit to believe in Him as a living God, as a God who answers prayer, and upon whose heart He lays a burden from which no rest can be found except in importunate crying unto God.

May God use this book to arouse many others to pray that the greatly-needed revival may come, and come speedily.

LET US PRAY.

COSIMO is a specialty publisher of books and publications that inspire, inform and engage readers. Our mission is to offer unique books to niche audiences around the world.

COSIMO CLASSICS offers a collection of distinctive titles by the great authors and thinkers throughout the ages. At COSIMO CLASSICS timeless classics find a new life as affordable books, covering a variety of subjects including: *Biographies, Business, History, Mythology, Personal Development, Philosophy, Religion and Spirituality,* and much more!

COSIMO-on-DEMAND publishes books and publications for innovative authors, non-profit organizations and businesses. COSIMO-on-DEMAND specializes in bringing books back into print, publishing new books quickly and effectively, and making these publications available to readers around the world.

COSIMO REPORTS publishes public reports that affect your world: from global trends to the economy, and from health to geo-politics.

FOR MORE INFORMATION CONTACT US AT
INFO@COSIMOBOOKS.COM

If you are a book-lover interested in our current catalog of books.

If you are an author who wants to get published

If you represent an organization or business seeking to reach your members, donors or customers with your own books and publications

COSIMO BOOKS ARE ALWAYS AVAILABLE AT ONLINE BOOKSTORES

VISIT COSIMOBOOKS.COM
BE INSPIRED, BE INFORMED

Printed in the United States
120646LV00001B/55/A